Wildfire

SUNY Series in Israeli Studies

Russell Stone, Editor

Wildfire

Grassroots Revolts in Israel in the Post-Socialist Era

Sam N. Lehman-Wilzig

State University of New York Press

Published by
State University of New York Press, Albany

For information, address State University of New York
Press, State University Plaza, Albany, N.Y. 12246

Production by M. R. Mulholland
Marketing by Dana E. Yanulavich

Library of Congress Cataloging-in-Publication Data

Lehman-Wilzig, Sam N.
    Wildfire : grassroots revolts in Israel in the post-Socialist era
/ Sam Lehman-Wilzig.
        p.   cm. —   (SUNY series in Israeli studies)
    Includes bibliographical references and indexes.
    ISBN 0–7914–0871–X — ISBN 0–7914–0872–8 (pbk.)
    1. Political participation—Israel. 2. Israel—Politics and
government. 3. Bureaucracy—Israel. I. Title. II. Series.
JQ1825.P359L46   1992
323' .042'095694—dc20
                                                                90–26930
                                                                CIP

10 9 8 7 6 5 4 3 2 1

This book is dedicated
to my two sons
Boaz and Avihai

May their present behavioral "revolt"
be channeled in useful social directions
as they grow to manhood

Contents

Acknowledgments

It is customary to thank colleagues, friends, and relatives for the aid offered in writing and completing a book. I will do so shortly. Less usual is an expression of acknowledgment to a city and specific political environment, but in this case it is altogether warranted.

As a citizen and resident of Israel since 1977, I have become accustomed and inured to its unique way of conducting public business. While this is a psychological defense mechanism of obvious social survival value, it does tend to undermine one's professional ability to perceive just how unusual Israel really is. My sabbatical sojourn in San Diego enabled me to put things in their proper perspective. Of course, no one would dare argue that Southern California is "representative" of the United States or Western Civilization as a whole. However, its laidback lifestyle, relatively low-key politics, and generally successful societal functioning, placed in stark contrast the Israeli way of life. The two stood on opposite extremes, throwing Israeli political dysfunction and social "chaos" into sharp relief for me.

For the opportunity to spend a year at San Diego State University, I am deeply beholden to my colleagues in the Lipinsky Institute for Contemporary Judaic Affairs, who invited me as their Annual Visiting Israeli Scholar. Special thanks go to Prof. Laurie Baron (and his gracious wife Bonnie), and his extremely efficient associate Barbara London, not only for their professional help but even more for their social solicitude in helping my family overcome the sociocultural "gap" between the Middle East and the Southwest. Beyond this book, their friendship is the most important product of my year in the California southland.

To be sure, the difficulty of uprooting home and hearth of which my wife bore the brunt, is no less deeply appreciated. A two-career marriage can cause hardship when one of the professional careers must be put on hold. I hope that this book can in some way mitigate the pain of the sacrifice which she bore.

Being so far geographically from the source of the book's subject matter was itself a problem. Thus, I am most thankful to the following colleagues and friends for their help in reading parts of the manuscript

as well as ferreting out additional information inaccessible to me in
California: Prof. Bernard Susser, Dr. Gerald Steinberg, Dr. Giora Gold-
berg, Dr. Meir Ungar, Dr. Adi Schnitzer, Dr. Eli Rekhess, and Mrs.
Reva Garmise.

Finally, my thanks to three journals—*Present Tense*, *Midstream*,
and *The Freeman*—for publishing earlier three of my articles which
dealt with the theme of this book in exploratory fashion. The support
of their editors, Murray Polner, Murray Zuckoff, and Brian Summers,
encouraged me in the belief that this topic would find an interested
audience. What you, as that audience, think of the book, however, is
entirely my responsibility and not theirs. They bear my thanks; I bear
all other critiques.

Introduction

Background

This book is an outgrowth of a study which I undertook in the 1980s regarding public protest in Israel, subsequently published as *Stiff-Necked People, Bottle-Necked System: The Evolution and Roots of Israeli Public Protest, 1949–1986*. While that work concentrated on the extremely high levels of extra-parliamentary activity found in Israel, it occurred to me that such civic action was but one example of a far larger phenomenon extending into virtually every significant facet of Israeli life. Thus was born the idea for the present study, which attempts to describe and analyze the origins and especially the manifestations of a truly remarkable sea change in Israeli public behavior. Its earliest expression can be found in three articles of mine, which appeared in Jewish general interest magazines (Lehman-Wilzig 1988, 15–19; 1989, 9–12; 1990a, 144–148). This book is a fuller and far more elaborate analysis of the entire subject.

There are at least three aspects of the general phenomenon towards which the grassroots revolts have been addressed (the fourth, intense bureaucratization, is basically incorporated within the other three). To be sure, they are deeply connected from a psychological and practical standpoint, but still constitute differing sides of a general coin. They bear defining at this introductory stage.

Definitions

Paternalism is that governing habit of mind that views the masses ("public" or "citizenry" would be giving the people too much credit, in the leaders' eyes) as being intrinsically incapable of leading their lives in a manner which would be to their own benefit. It essentially views government as the "guardian" of political neophytes who must be led as much as possible in the pursuit of their happiness, for left alone they would tend to make serious personal decision-making errors.

While paternalism is a frame of mind normally found in autocratic and/or backward societies, it may exist as well in a modern democracy. The two are not necessarily contradictory, for democracy is the system through which the leaders are selected and says little of their leadership style. In fact, some degree of governmental paternalism can be found even in the most advanced nations. For example, the American system of food stamps for the poor (instead of granting them extra cash to make the purchasing decision by themselves) is intrinsically paternalistic. Nevertheless, as this example suggests, in certain cases a measure of governmental paternalism may actually be called for, given the proven (in)ability of the specific population group to make the rationally or "morally correct" choice by, and for, themselves.

Thus, governmental paternalism is not in and of itself wrong or impolitic; just as parents need to be paternalistic with their children, so, too, government at times. However, kids do grow up, and as time goes by parents understand that it is necessary and healthy for the offspring to increasingly make their own decisions. When government does not loosen the reins, when the "guardianship" continues *ad infinitum*, problems arise and its ostensible charges begin to revolt. In short, no specific dose of paternalism can be said to be wise or unwise, correct or incorrect, but if the degree and extent of paternalistic government is too great over a lengthy period of time, the system will suffer from societal turbulence and political instability—not to mention economic stagnation.

Socialism is the economic system in which paternalism tends to be expressed the most. This is so from two different standpoints. First, in the socialist system it is the state that concentrates the means of production (and services) in its hands, in order to more "rationally distribute" the national wealth. The assumption here is that working as individuals, the public at large is generally incapable of producing wealth in maximal fashion, and that without government ownership and control, most private citizens would be at a loss to support themselves and their families.

Second, socialism also entails high rates of taxation in order to fund a wide-ranging network of welfare services. Little need be added here on the detrimental effect to the work incentive that high taxes cause. Taxation is corrosive of private freedom of action not so much in channeling work in a certain direction, but rather in dampening the will to work, i.e. in engendering an environment in which economic sloth might well be the most rational decision!

More of an explanation is needed regarding the "problem" inherent in the welfare services provided. In and of itself there is nothing wrong with public charity, but it does tend to breed a dependency on government and dampen private initiative (not only in the economic sense of the term, but in the wider life cycle sense of taking one's fate into one's own hands). This is due to the fact, as we just saw, that such a policy is usually carried out in broad fashion, not taking into account differences in needs and desires of the populace. To continue our food example from the Israeli case, heavy subsidization of certain basic commodities tends to influence almost the entire population to purchase those goods which are cheaper by government fiat, rather than the foods which they would have purchased had they been given a free economic choice. All this, of course, is in addition to the most obvious flaw in the socialist system: rampant waste and misallocation of scarce resources.

Centralism ensues from paternalism and socialism, in that it is the overwhelmingly preferred institutional mode of carrying out such a general governance philosophy and economic system. In order to ensure that only "those in the know" determine policy, and in order to guarantee the authorities' dominance of economic control, the system of government inevitably tends to concentrate political power at the apex of the pyramid. All significant decisions are funneled to the central leadership, which then decides what is permissible for the public to do and what measure of economic and social freedom will be allowed to the citizenry.

Once again, centralism is not necessarily antidemocratic, and in certain institutions and circumstances is even quite necessary (e.g. the army, which in Israel paradoxically is one of the least paternalistic of all the country's public institutions—one of the reasons why it has been the most successful). Here, too, there exists a chronological relativity, with centralism being more germane in an early period of general instability or social homogeneity than in a later era of order and/or social pluralism. The greater the institutionalization of society and the more pluralistic it becomes, the greater the possibility (and need) for decentralized decision making. As we shall see in the following chapters, what was useful during the pre-State *yishuv* period became progressively dysfunctional as time and circumstances changed in a more modern and heterogeneous State of Israel.

These three elements, then, are distinctly interrelated—socialism as an ideological *weltanschauung* is expressed through paternalism and centralism as behavioral and institutional manifestations. Therefore, no attempt will be made here to artificially compartmentalize them in our analysis of Israel's grassroots revolts. As the Israeli public views the matter in wholistic fashion and does not stand too closely on the finely nuanced differences of the general phenomenon, neither shall we.

Why Wildfire?

A few additional words are in order regarding the title of the book. Aside from its being somewhat eye-catching, there are several reasons for the choice of *Wildfire*. First, wildfire usually has no specific origin—at least that is known to us. While chapter 1 will analyze the nature of the Israeli "forest" from which this social conflagration emanates, and chapter 3 enumerates the earliest signs of its outbreak, this is not a phenomenon that has any single source—ergo, the plural "revolts" in the subtitle.

Second, and related to this, is the fact that wildfire equally has no set boundaries. Indeed, its most notable characteristic lies precisely in that it ends up engulfing not merely the original "forest" but spreading beyond its natural habitat—in our Israeli case, beyond the purely political realm. This is not an issue-specific, nor even an area-of-life-specific phenomenon.

Third, and finally, wildfire moves very quickly and arrives in many cases without the victims being aware of it until it is too late. As we shall see, despite some early warning signals in the 1970s, the phenomenon discussed in this book took much of Israeli society by surprise in the 1980s, leaping from one issue area to another with alacrity. In a mere ten years, an entire philosophical system of control, governance, and rule lay under attack—and in many cases in ruins, or at the least in disorderly retreat in the face of this raging social onslaught. In sum, *wildfire* bespeaks of amorphous origins, comprehensive scope, and rapid movement—precisely the environmental elements found in Israel's several grassroots revolts.

Antecedent Works

This is not the first work to touch on certain aspects of the phenomenon. For example, Sprinzak (1986) describes what he calls the rise of "illegalism" in Israel. Technically he is correct, for many of the things to be described in the present book *are* illegal in the narrow sense of the term.

However, there are two things missing from his seminal analysis. First, of the four illegalism archetypes he describes, three relate to the political establishment, and the fourth involves the public's behavior in a narrow political sense, i.e. unlawful protest demonstrations and terrorism (Sprinzak 1986, 24–25). As will be argued, this is far too restrictive a perspective to take.

Second, Sprinzak does not indicate that there may be an underlying need for such anormative behavior on the part of the Israeli public. In other words, while he puts the "blame" on the peculiar culture and psyche of Jewish Israelis, there is nowhere a sense that there may be deep-rooted systemic reasons leading Israelis to behave in the way they have come to behave over the past two decades. This is not to say that Jews do not have any sort of different political culture; I myself have argued that part of the Israeli protest phenomenon lies in the traditionally Jewish ethic of "oppositionism" (Lehman-Wilzig 1991b), and Sprinzak devotes quite a lot of attention to the "cultural" element as well. The book before you, however, will try to make it clear that the matter goes much farther than that.

Yishai's recent pathbreaking study of Israeli voluntarism (1987) has also added a brick to this edifice. However, here too the author did not deal with the cause (or original facilitator) of the problem, but rather with the most recent instance of the Israeli public's determination to institutionalize grassroots action. To be sure, this is a most welcome development as it should serve to channel Israelis' extrainstitutional energies in a more orderly and nondestabilizing direction. This too will be discussed in the book.

For her part, Danet's ongoing study of Israeli *proteksia* (1988) has shown just how "institutionalized" Israeli anti-institutionalism has become when dealing with the formal bureaucratic system. The use of friends, relatives, and social acquaintances in positions of power or authority to pry open closed bureaucratic doors has been the classic Israeli way of doing public business. While it was the first (and for some, still the preferred) way of beating the system, it has generally been an extremely circumspect tool, i.e. utilized behind the scenes and away from the public eye.

What sets most of the phenomena discussed in this book apart from *proteksia* is their more public nature, a sort of collective "coming out of the closet" on the part of the increasingly restive Israeli populace: quasi-public trade in Black Dollars, openly public use of school premises, conspiratorially public laying of illegal cable television wires, etc. The revolt is now far more brazen, seeking to circumvent not just bureaucratic barriers, but to undermine the system and influence the reform of actual official public policy and legislation.

This also suggests another key difference between the phenomenon that Danet describes and the array of activities described in the present book. While she notes the use of "universalistic" as well as "particularistic" channels for redressing grievances (the State Ombudsman is an example of the former, *proteksia* of the latter), her focus is exclusively on what goes on within the formal system of gov-

6 *Introduction*

ernment. The description (and analysis) is very good as far as it goes, but it hardly goes far enough; given that the underlying public policy of the system, and not just its effectiveness in producing the mandated output, is in serious discordance with what the public wants along a host of issue areas, the inevitable next step has been to bypass the bureaucratic system altogether. It is this latter, relatively more recent phenomenon, to which the present study is addressed (as I explain at greater length below).

Most recently, Ben-Yehuda (1989, 152–164) touched on a few of the areas discussed in part II of this book, in his interesting but highly schematic article (schematic, as he acknowldges by his subtitle: "Some Exploratory Notes"). Ben-Yehuda calls these "alternative systems," which at least has the advantage of suggesting some form of moral neutrality.

However, the use of "system" is problematic in that it suggests a full-blown institutional complex that has already arisen to replace the officially sanctioned one. This is both untrue and misleading in that the goal of Israelis participating in their respective grassroots revolts is not to establish other entire systems. Rather, the motive force is to supplement the existing ones as long as the latter continue not to function, and indirectly force the authorities to either reform theirs or to create other new ones to take their place.

Moreover, in the vast majority of the areas, which we shall cover in part II, there is very little in the way of a *systematically* organized structure competing with the officially sanctioned one. That is precisely why I call these "grassroots revolts": on the one hand, they are not institutional phenomena (hence "grassroots"); on the other hand, this is not a revolution whose goal is to supplant the official systems, but merely a "revolt" against the depredations of the present way of doing public business.

Purposes of This Work

There is an inevitable question which emerges from the foregoing: why the paucity of research and discussion of this overall Israeli phenomenon? The answer leads us beyond the narrow confines of the subject and beyond even the country itself.

Most political science researchers—around the world, but especially in Israel—tend to concentrate on the *formal* system of power relationships. Indeed, even those interested in "oppositionist" activity almost always view matters from the perspective of how citizens on the "outs" (i.e. powerless, seriously alienated, highly dissatisfied) band together to enhance their own power in the inevitable frontal clash with the authorities (e.g. Yishai's work). Thus, there is a whole subdiscipline comprising reams of books on pressure groups, interest groups, extra-electoral political participation, political mobilization, opposition movements and parties, etc.

To take but one example, Janice Perlman's pioneering survey of American community groups (1979, 403–425) was entitled "Grass-rooting the System." She noted that in the American case, "the lessons of the sixties have served the seventies in good stead…[as] the thrust of the seventies is on local organizations and on issues which are more rooted in people's daily lives" (Perlman 1979, 405–406).

As just noted above, however, the Israeli case proceeded differently. While here too there was a period of mass protest (the seventies), the next stage in the eighties (which constitutes the subject matter of this book) did not involve *organized*, local grassroots development, but rather nationwide—yet mostly *noninstitutionalized*—activity by innumerable Israelis, which in effect had a decisive (albeit largely unintentional) collective impact on the polity.

Why the difference between the American and the Israeli cases? The argument will be made later on that the Israeli public was reacting in the most optimal fashion given the nature of the country's system, which does not hold the public's representatives electorally accountable—in contradistinction to America's district system of representation. Indeed, this is the reason that after a decade of anomic "revolts," the latest grassroots movement (one of the more organized in the Israeli milieu) has finally addressed the problem of the political system itself (chapter 10).

Which brings us back to the question of prior research. In Israel, precisely because of the even greater importance and power of the central political apparatus (relative to all other democracies), the research has tended to focus almost exclusively on the system and its formal actors and processes: parties, Knesset, bureaucracy, elections, etc. Even my own earlier work, although concentrating on antisystem processes and phenomena, did not venture far from such a closed systemic perspective: collective public protest by Israel's citizens against the policies of the government, i.e. extraparliamentary activity *addressed to* the parliamentary system.

Again, precisely because the Israeli political system is so all-encompassing, and because it is so difficult to change the Israeli government's basic policy through even strong extra-parliamentary pressure (Lehman-Wilzig 1990b, 113–119), the Israeli public moved to a form of "protest" that is far more amorphous and almost completely

devoid of political "formalism"—what I define here as Israel's "grassroots revolts." Indeed, this is so much the case that most commentators who have touched on different aspects of the general phenomenon outlined in this book do not perceive them as being part of
a larger whole, or even in most cases (the exceptions being chapters 4
and 10) as being "political activity" *per se.* I contend that this is a serious misreading of the situation.

Thus, especially because Israeli politics has so heavily influenced social and economic life in Israel, I would like to suggest that
social and economic public (mis)behavior must be recognized not
only as intrinsically political but as affecting and changing public
(political) policy. In a few issue areas such a motive is quite conscious
among the Israelis; in many others, it is not conscious at all. But the
specific motivation or conscious goal of the public is not what should
lead us here; rather, it is the ultimate effect which is crucial—intended
or unintended.

In short, in addition to its obvious purpose of describing and
analyzing a very interesting and significant phenomenon in Israeli
society, this book also has the intent of broadening the intellectual
and research scope of what constitutes "politics" in Israel (and by
extension, the world). Chapter 13 will devote some serious attention
to this point. Not that the public's intent is necessarily "revolutionary"—after all, if democracy means "power to the people," then
almost all public activity of the citizenry should have been defined
from the start as "political." That this is generally not the case in the
present day and age is but one indication of how far we have come in
reifying representative democracy and its sundry institutions. Politics—even (and in the future, *especially*) democratic politics—should
not be so circumscribed.

The Problem of Value Perspective

Many readers—especially those of Anglo-Saxon culture, if not
provenance—will be appalled at several of the things described in
this book. I have strived throughout to be as "neutral" as possible in
analyzing the various elements of the subject without apportioning
moral blame. Nevertheless, two things should be kept in mind.

First, notwithstanding the ethical fault to be found (or not to be
found), it is obvious that from a social standpoint many of these public activities are seriously destabilizing to the fabric of society, especially if left unchallenged or unresponded to by the authorities. As
will be noted, the good news here is that in many cases the Israeli

government has reacted in positive fashion by fixing, or at least ameliorating, the problems. The bad news, though, is that such behavior can easily become ingrained and transfer itself to other walks of life where continued social damage may ensue.

Second, and conversely, precisely because the official system (whether political, economic, or whatever) has functioned in such poor fashion, the grassroots revolts in Israel may have been the only—and probably the most effective—way of forcing significant long-term change. Thus, while chaotic and even potentially dangerous in the short term, Israel's grassroots revolts taken together can be viewed as a bloodless revolution for significant positive reform.

For the average Western reader, then (except perhaps the Italians—Danet 1989, 174), the contemporary Israeli domestic situation will probably seem like a chapter out of Alice in Wonderland. For those who are actually familiar with Israeli life, the true picture is more one of a society that works—albeit in somewhat skewed fashion. By weeding out some of the more deleterious aspects of these grassroots revolts, Israel may ultimately come to resemble most other normal Western societies—for better or for worse.

Part I

Background

1

The Spark: Zionism, Socialism, and Governmental Paternalism

Origins

From the very start, modern Zionism could not be classified as a grassroots movement. Unlike the waves of mass Jewish immigration from Eastern Europe to the United States, which were relatively spontaneous movements of indigent people taking fate into their own hands without any guiding philosophy, the Zionist movement was initiated and led from on high: Eastern intellectuals and writers (Pinsker and Smolenskin); Western journalists, scientists, and philanthropists (Herzl, Weizmann, and Rothschild). Thus was established the pattern for nation building in the new-old state from the start.

This is not to suggest that the early Zionist pioneers were forced to emigrate to Palestine. One must distinguish between the original pioneering urge, which was quite voluntaristic, and the way matters developed for them once in the Promised Land. Zionist *khalutziut* (pioneering) had within it two components—the free choice decision to go to *Eretz Yisrael*, and a tremendous amount of self-sacrifice after one's arrival in Palestine in order to further the collective Zionist good. While the first element was highly individualistic, such individualism generally ceased at the port of entry; the specific type and degree of self-sacrifice was more often than not decided from above— be it by the patronal Baron de Rothschild during the First Aliyah, or the shirtsleeved socialist apparatchiks of the third and subsequent periods of mass immigration.

The Second Aliyah (1904–1913) set the general approach in institutional concrete. Virtually all these early pioneers came from the hotbed of revolutionary socialist Russia and Eastern Europe—Ben-Gurion, Ben-Zvi, Katznelson—with an ideological zeal and fervent belief in the need for centralized control and direction that only the formerly powerless can muster. In the social, economic, and especially political *tabula rasa* that was Palestine, they proceeded to evolve a system of top-to-bottom paternalism, which would be the hallmark of the entire pre-State *yishuv* period and the first two decades of the post-State era as well.

This is not to suggest that these Zionist founding fathers were interested in power for its own sake. Not only did they truly believe in the rightness and efficacy of this top-to-bottom approach, but to a large extent the circumstances in Palestine warranted—perhaps even demanded—it. On the one hand, the early Zionist pioneers were almost universally without substantial personal economic resources (very few European Jews with means would even consider leaving their cultured home for the primitivity of Ottoman Palestine). On the other hand, unlike the situation in the American West, there weren't even any indigenous natural resources in Palestine to work with either. As a result, there wasn't much choice for the early Zionist leadership but to husband and maximally exploit whatever came to hand—through an organized and collective effort.

These two factors, socialist ideology and circumstantial need, provided a powerful justification for Zionist paternalism. What set the early Zionist pioneers apart from other national founders was their ability to perceive that such an approach could not be dependent solely on their heroic efforts and national visionary will. Rather, they set out early on to institutionalize Zionist paternalism through a host of organizations within and outside the *yishuv*.

Developing Institutions to Institutionalize Development

The most obvious and ultimately most effective such institution was the political party. Obvious, because the party was the central means of mass mobilization in the socialist revolutionary tradition. Having been socialized within this hotbed of European political action during their youthful years, the pioneer settlers accepted as axiomatic the need to establish a political party.

But what sort of party? Here, too, their earlier revolutionary experience suggested that to be fully successful it would not only have to involve itself in simple vote gathering but in ideological indoctrination as well. Classic Marxist theory viewed politics as but one element of a larger economic totality. In order to establish a just society, it would not suffice to merely wield the levers of political power; rather, no less than complete socioeconomic remodeling and a concomitant remaking of the Jew was called for. Put simply, the "normalization of the Jewish economic profile"—away from the overemphasis on commerce, finance, and intellectual pursuits, and towards agricultural and industrial manual labor—was the order of the day.

How was this to be accomplished? The Zionist political party would have to become a "full-service" institution, not only offering political leadership but a full range of economic, social, and political services as well. Ironically enough, the historical source for such a full-service approach was none other than the local Jewish communal governments in the Diaspora. The *shtetl* in Poland, for example not only etymologically meant "little state" but conducted itself like one—providing and/or establishing virtually all the local Jews' social, economic, cultural, and political needs and institutions: taxes, wage and price regulations, courts, schools, synagogues, welfare funds, sickhouses, etc. (Elazar 1981, 23–63).

Origins notwithstanding, the Zionist parties were but the first step along this old/new road in the Jews' new/old home. By predating the first official Jewish communal government in the *yishuv* by a decade or so (not to mention the State of Israel by close to fifty years), it was the early socialist political parties that set the tone for what was expected of the powers-that-be—whether party, government, or labor federation. Once it came into being, the government could hardly do less for the Zionist public than the political parties were attempting. In any event, as the socialist camp came to dominate the communal government from the start of the British Mandatory period, it made little difference which specific organ of rule was actually providing the services. The critical point was that the Palestine Zionist public, no less than the Jewish leadership, took it for granted that such political/governmental services would run the gamut.

Aiding the Second Aliyah leaders were the immigrants who came in the Third Aliyah of the 1920s. Many of these were politically capable (and highly educated) socialists from middle class backgrounds who found themselves outside the Bolshevik Revolution when it turned against Zionism in 1922. Upon their arrival in Palestine they didn't seek laborer jobs, but rather hooked into the Labor party (Ahdut Ha'avodah and Ha'shomer Ha'tza'ir, at the time) or Histadrut labor federation positions. Yonathan Shapira aptly describes this symbiotic relationship and its consequences:

> The veterans needed a party apparatus and the newcomers were willing and able to build it. The newcomers, at the same time, were willing to follow the lead of the older leaders. Their arrival as refugees from Soviet Russia may have contributed to their deference to the veteran leaders.... These two groups—the top

leaders at the helm of the party and the Histadrut, and the apparatus builders—in cooperation managed to organize and direct
the masses (Shapira 1986, 183–184).

To be sure, strong central government was a real necessity not
only given the economic exigencies of the period but also due to the
tenuous political circumstances in which the nascent Zionist movement found itself. Notwithstanding the early sympathetic stance of
His Majesty's government as embodied in the 1917 Balfour Declaration, it became clear soon thereafter that the Jewish State would not be
born in the normal and "inevitable" course of events. British Middle
East interests, coupled with (and sympathetic to) violent Arab antipathy to Zionism, meant that the Zionist authorities would need to
exhibit as strong and unified a front as possible. In the best of national
circumstances, "foreign policy" is the prerogative of the executive
branch; in the *yishuv*'s far more precarious and sensitive diplomatic
situation, centralized decisionmaking was absolutely imperative. The
circle was thus complete: both on the "domestic" plane as well as the
external front the *yishuv*'s leadership called the shots.

The irony of all this, then, was that the Mandate policy—both in
its initial and later phases—actually aided the *yishuv* in its drive
towards political consolidation. As a result of the Balfour Declaration,
the Jews as well as the Arabs of Palestine were allowed, even encouraged, to develop their own communal institutions once it became
clear that the two sides could not and would not do so jointly (the
Arabs never accomplished this, for reasons that need not concern us
here). Thus, despite not having sovereign control over their destiny,
the Jews of Palestine in fact had a large measure of political autonomy
without at first having to devote any significant economic resources
to internal policing and external national defense.

By the time British policy shifted against the *yishuv* in the 1930s,
the quasi-governmental institutions were already well in place; at that
point, the new British policy only served to redouble the Zionists' efforts
in mobilizing all their governmental resources for the struggle ahead. As
a recent scholar of the period put it: "The British...presented the Zionists
with a near optimal mix of positive and negative policies to help
increase the capabilities of para-statal organizations" (Migdal 1989, 12).

The Lack of Institutional Counterweight

None of this is to suggest that the system which developed was
fundamentally undemocratic. Far from it, for the number of parties

that won seats in the Jewish communal legislature was beyond anything usually found in preindependent times, let alone normal political periods. Nor was there anything approaching universal "consensual" agreement in the *yishuv*, within the broad socialist camp and especially between that camp and the Revisionists on the right. Nevertheless, despite these ideological and political cleavages, two factors mitigated against any early diminution of the overall centralized and paternalistic approach.

First, virtually all the parties (with the exception of the Liberal/Progressive camp) took the same "full service" tack towards their respective constituencies (to the extent possible, given the limited economic means of each). And how could it be otherwise? In order to have any hope of competing with Mapai and her satellite coalition partners (all of whom had the added advantage of controlling the levers of the Jewish communal government), other parties could not be perceived as lagging in their array of sociocultural offerings. Hence, the spectacle of party-owned and/or controlled newspapers, publishing houses, health plans, athletic teams, banks, insurance companies, etc., etc.

Second, if there was to be a real challenge to such socialistic paternalism, it would have had to come from the Revisionist side. However, while from a socioeconomic ideological standpoint Jabotinsky's party did indeed issue a challenge of sorts, the very *style* of revisionist rule—at its extremes bordering on the fascist, almost always authoritarian (despite Jabotinsky's own liberal proclivities)—merely reinforced the general air of top-to-bottom governance. The two major Zionist blocs, then, neatly complemented each other from this perspective: the socialists through their party organization, the Revisionists by way of their approach to political leadership. As we shall see further on in this book, it is no coincidence that the greatest demise of Israeli governmental paternalism occurred not after 1977 upon the fall of the Labor establishment (although that was certainly a major domino), but rather in the mid 1980s, only after the last of Israel's "strong" leaders—Menachem Begin—exited the political arena.

Unholy Trinity:
Labor Party, Laborious Government, Laboring Union

How did the socialist camp manage to stay in power for so long? The answer to that question provides still another factor behind the paternalistic stranglehold in which Israeli society was kept. The Labor bloc worked on not one (party), not two (government), but no less than three different but interrelated planes. The third leg of this all-encompassing rule was, of course, the giant labor federation called the Histadrut. As a normal trade union, it would have been sufficient to significantly buttress Mapai's power. However, the Histadrut became far more than a simple trade union federation.

To begin with, it ultimately came to represent some 85 percent of Israel's salaried workforce—far and away a record among the world's democracies (by comparison, in labor's heyday in the United States less than a third of the country's workforce was unionized). However, due to the very difficult unemployment situation in which the *yishuv* occasionally found itself, this labor federation decided to do the heretofore unthinkable (except, perhaps, in Karl Marx's utopian dreams)—establish companies in order to guarantee employment to the arriving masses!

This only served to further ensure the perpetuation of Israeli public paternalism—in two different ways. First and foremost, the worker was now afforded yet another public address for economic beneficence; in fact, the Histadrut soon came to have virtual monopolistic control over the employment bureaus. As a result, a job seeker had little choice but to turn to the Histadrut when in search of a salaried position, and more often than not would find such work within the Histadrut's corporate alter ego. Once in, of course, the full panoply of Histadrut/Mapai indoctrination and services would be brought to bear. Whether directly or indirectly, a very significant portion of Israel's workers eventually found themselves in the comfortable bosom of Big Union.

Second, and concomitantly, whereas in most other societies of the early twentieth century the union camp at times constituted the sole major counterforce to government power, in Palestine and later Israel the Histadrut by so closely aligning itself—ideologically *and* institutionally—with the *yishuv*'s Labor government, effectively took away from the working class any possibility of organizationally opposing overbearing government.

Worse yet, by burning both ends of the candle—as the employees' sole representative, and as the employer even in the late eighties of 18 percent of the national workforce (Rabushka & Hanke 1989, 13)—the Histadrut undercut its own primary role as steadfast guardian of the workers' rights. The perception (and occasional reality) of such a conflict of interest further undermined any possibility of an unalloyed ally of society's weaker strata.

Most startling, and almost forgotten in the mythology of early Zionist history, is the fact that if the most dominant personality on the

Labor scene—David Ben-Gurion—had had his way, the extent of paternalistic control and domination of the entire *yishuv* by the Labor/Histadrut alliance would have been even greater. The following description (coupled with Ben-Gurion's own quotes) by one of his sympathetic biographers is important not only for its explicit prescriptions, but because it offers us a glimpse into the mindset of Israel's premier founding father and first prime minister, who more than anyone else set the tone for governance in the emerging Jewish State (despite the occasional opposition of even his own Labor colleagues):

> In the early 1920s, Ben-Gurion advanced the following proposal: to convert the Histadrut into a workers corporation, "...an egalitarian commune of all the workers of Palestine under military discipline...[that would] take over all the farms and urban cooperatives, the wholesale supplies of the entire working community, and the direction and conduct of all public works in the country."

> In face of the fiercely critical reaction and the accusations of "Bolshevik" and "dogmatic" tendencies, Ben-Gurion was obliged to withdraw the proposal. He submitted a new plan that omitted such concepts as "military discipline," but this too was rejected by some of the Histadrut leaders. Finally he presented the Histadrut with a third plan that was far more moderate and prudent...the Workers Corporation, to which every member of the Histadrut would *automatically* [my emphasis; S.L-W.] belong and to which the Histadrut would entrust the administration of all its financial and cooperative enterprises to "direct its activities toward the needs of all the workers" (Bar-Zohar 1978, 50).

Israeli socialist paternalism, then, turns out to have been the more *moderate* alternative to Bolshevist Zionism—the actual early preferred choice of the nation's central political leader.

External Paternalism

As noted above, the resources found in early Palestine—of both the immigrants and the land itself—were exceptionally meager. In effect, this meant that still another layer of paternalism had to be added to the situation, above and beyond those Jewish communal institutions established in the *yishuv*. These were the external World Zionist Organization (WZO) and its later adjunct the Jewish Agency.

The ruling tone was set by the founder of modern Political Zionism, Theodore Herzl. A highly cultured and well-to-do Budapest/Viennese Jew, Herzl (unlike his ideological opponent Ahad Ha'am) had the prescience to understand that Zionism could only succeed if it looked to the Jewish masses—and not to the still all-too-comfortable middle class, or the intelligentsia—as the main source of *aliyah* to Palestine. Yet, Herzl was too much the refined gentleman to place much faith in the ability of such lower class *hoi polloi* to manage the difficult task of nation building by themselves. It would be up to him, and similar Zionist luminaries—genteel Dr. Chaim Weizmann the scientist, haughty Dr. Max Nordau, prominent Heidelberg Prof. Hermann Schapiro (the proposer of the Jewish National Fund), industrial tycoons Alexander Marmorek (vice president of the WZO) and Max Bodenheimer, *et al*—to plan and forge the path (financially and politically, not personally of course) for the Children of Israel's return to the Promised Land. Even the socialist leaders within the WZO, e.g. Nahman Syrkin, were not truly of the working class (although assiduously laboring for the workers); the model of benign Leninist leadership seemed to be their guiding political *modus operandi,* as Ben-Gurion acknowledged explicitly on at least one occasion (Avi-hai 1974, 286).

The setting up of the Jewish Agency in 1929 established a new level of "Zionist paternalism," ultimately serving as a precedent for "sugar daddyism" of the worst order. It was one thing to have avowed Zionists paying the piper and calling the tune of nation building in the *yishuv;* it was quite another matter to have professed non-Zionists funding the enterprise.

That the Jewish Agency would soon be operationally taken over by the Zionist functionaries was beside the point; the idea and reality of constant reliance on external sources of funding (not merely external to Palestine/Israel, but to the Zionist movement as a whole) was the surest sign that the nascent Jewish State was becoming addicted to outside help. From Jewish Agency fundraising in the thirties and forties, to substantial German reparations in the fifties and sixties (and now once again from former East Germany in the nineties), and on to massive American foreign aid in the seventies and eighties, the pattern is all of the same piece in principle. Not only were the Zionist masses beholden to their leaders, but those same leaders carried matters one step further by becoming financially hooked on non-Zionist sources of aid.

Once again, this may have been unavoidable (and some would argue, continues to be unavoidable) given the dire financial straits in which the Zionist movement and the State of Israel have continually found themselves. None of this is to impute some nefarious plot by the authorities—Israeli, Zionist, or non-Zionist—to control the whole enterprise out of any lust for power or financial gain. In almost all cases, objective needs for such an approach did exist in at least some measure, and certainly could be rationally justified in the context of an unusual and quite difficult situation.

Whatever the "moral" balance of credit/blame, however, one thing becomes clear in hindsight. Despite the relatively democratic nature of the *yishuv*'s (and later Israel's) election system, there was little actual grassroots democratic activity—not to mention personal freedom of choice—in evidence anywhere else in a system nurtured and directed from the top. By 1948, the pattern of top-to-bottom decisionmaking had been firmly set: in the founding of new settlements, building of industrial factories, development of academic universities, the territorial dispersal of new immigrants, and even the establishment of local government councils.

Pre-1948: Variables Leading Invariably to Paternalism

Overall, then, the factors underlying pre-Israel's development of a highly centralized, socialistically paternalistic, "strong" system of government were many. Whereas other "new states" coming into being in the twentieth century had to contend with a multitude of political actors and factors which tended to reduce the power of the rulers (at least from the standpoint of social control), several specific circumstances in the Zionist case enabled the rulers to increase and broaden their social control over the Jewish population. In analyzing the "crystallization of the state" and the absence of sources which usually tend to weaken the power of the emerging elite, Migdal (1989, 25) enumerates the most salient elements, most of which were noted at some length above. His conclusion aptly sums up our pre-State discussion as well:

> In the case of Israel, an unusual number of exogenous factors neutralized and weakened the negative effects of old rulemakers, potential new rulemakers, and possible statebreakers on state consolidation. The overall weakness of actors in these three categories in actually challenging for social control coupled with the labor Zionists' fear of the potential damage some of these actors could do resulted in an unusual opportunity for the Israeli state to build a relatively high level of social control and capabilities. These factors include: 1) the weakening impact of

migration on old strategies of survival among Jews; 2) the weaknesses of potential local and all-Palestine rivals, both among the Jews and Arabs; 3) the willingness of British leaders of the mandatory state to grant significant autonomy; 4) the availability of skillful cadres, who did not exact a high ideological price for their participation in the state-in-making; 5) the willingness of elements in the World Zionist movement to work for diplomatic support and to channel significant material support to the Yishuv without exacting a high ideological or organizational price; 6) the relatively limited negative effects of the destruction of war on the ability to offer strategies of survival and the positive effects of the threat of war on inducing increased mobilization; and 7) the existence of a power balance in the Middle East, which impeded the emergence of a statebreaking hegemony in the region.

If Israel was virtually unique among the twentieth century's newly independent countries in the smoothness of governmental transition and essential stability of its regime, this was due in no small measure to the centralized and unified power of its government apparatus. As we shall see later on, however, it would also prove to be the source further down the road of much of the State's greatest domestic headache—a veritable revolt against such overbearing leadership.

Mamlakhtiut: The Ideology and Practice of State Paternalism

If the general pattern of governmental paternalism was already firmly set by the time of independence, it still lacked one thing—an official ideology. This was provided by Prime Minister Ben-Gurion early on, in a policy which he called *mamlakhtiut*, "statism."

It was a measure of how much the Israeli public accepted the reality (and perhaps the need) for such centralization and paternalism, that Ben-Gurion had no qualms about declaratively and explicitly letting the cat out of the bag. From a personal-political perspective there was no need for him to do so, for he stood unchallenged as the fulcrum of the entire political system. Why then did he announce that the Israeli government would henceforth be guided by the principle of *mamlakhtiut*?

To a great degree, the answer lies in the first and most original brick of the entire paternalistic edifice noted earlier: the political parties. In the early 1950s they still wielded a huge amount of power, to the point of making governance difficult even for Ben-Gurion.

To take but one absurd example, the parties continued to demand that the masses of new immigrants be apportioned to the various parties by a "party key," with each party having first crack at indoctrinating and servicing its respective quota of new members within the Israeli "transit" camps. Not only was such a situation bizarre considering that most of these *olim* had not the foggiest notion of what a political party was or what it was supposed to do, but the socioeconomic and ideological makeup of these groups was wildly out of sync with the party key. For instance, whereas most of the parties were nonreligious (and not a few antireligious), the vast majority of the *edot ha'mizrakh* (Jews from Arab countries) who arrived immediately after Israel was established were fervently religious, with the rest religiously traditional at the least.

Thus, the very first socialization process these immigrants underwent was one of forced indoctrination, of expedited "modernization" in the parlance of the Israeli political establishment. The language here was quite explicit at times, as can be seen from the following statement by the head of the Jewish Agency's Culture Department: "our job and the job of the country is not to leave these (formerly) exiled people with their exile mentality, but rather to render them trustworthy partners in the great and noble Israeli revolution which has occurred" (Levitan 1983, 196).

Party-keyed immigrant absorption was but one of many problematic areas which threatened to cleave Israeli society asunder. There still existed several ideologically and party-oriented school streams in Israel, with the obvious potential of institutionalizing and perpetuating Israeli ideological factiousness. It was to avoid this threat of deepening societal cleavage that Ben-Gurion announced his policy of *mamlakhtiut*. Once again, however, while ostensibly warranted by the inherent dangers facing Israeli society, the actual effect was to deepen government centralization and the public's dependency on the institutions of government.

The clearest example of this was probably the relationship between Israel's central government and the municipalities. The Interior Ministry was given sole responsibility for the functioning of local government, and proceeded to do so with a heavyhandedness found only in authoritarian regimes. All local budgets had to be approved by the ministry which in any case provided more than 50 percent of the municipalities' operating revenue; local bylaws also had to be approved by the ministry, including any new forms of local taxation; and most unusual of all, the ministry had the authority—used on several occasions—to fire and replace the municipal council and mayor!

Such a governmental situation was especially insidious given that in Israel it is usually on the local level where one finds the fullest expression of grassroots activity and display of civic initiative. With the municipal councils' hands tied, however, there was little incentive for public political activity on the local level. In the event, it was not until the local election law was changed (direct election of the mayor in 1978), that local grassroots activity began to flourish. This was immediately crowned with the victory of many independent party lists, which already in 1978 collectively ruled over more local citizens than the Likud (Lehman-Wilzig 1982, 107)!

On the broader socioeconomic front, in the mid fifties the government began to take on an expanded role. If the central authorities had no choice but to place the masses of immigrants in transit camps catch-as-catch-can (because of the serious lack of housing), it was but a natural step to eventually move them out of those camps and decide for them that in the national interest they would be permanently settled in newly built "development towns" on the periphery—socially and geographically—of Israeli society.

Such a policy of forced exurbanization may have been at least partly justified at the time in terms of the country's need for population dispersal and settlement of very sparse areas (although almost all such development towns have by now proven to be economic failures). They certainly had the practical effect of increasing that population's overall dependency on the state's authorities.

To be sure, there was a certain trade-off inherent in Ben-Gurion's policy of *mamlakhtiut;* if the state's involvement in the citizens' lives increased, this would in no small part come at the expense of the parties themselves. Interestingly, but not altogether surprisingly, the greatest antagonism to the Prime Minister's policy came from within some parts of the socialist camp, as it had the most power to lose. Thus, for example, it was the Labor-oriented Palmach elite corps that argued most vociferously against its disbandment and wholesale integration into Zahal, the newly established Israeli Defense Forces (IDF) (Shapira 1985).

Why, then, did Ben-Gurion insist on upsetting his party's applecart? There can be no gainsaying his worry over the stability of the State, not to mention the need to bring a semblance of unity to the highly ideologically fractured society. By setting up one integrating army, by reducing the number of school systems to a minimum, etc., he hoped to change Israel from the chaotic Byzantine to the merely divided Levantine. On the other hand, there were two additional factors at play here as well.

Ben-Gurion had grave doubts that the Jews were ready for self-government (Cohen 1987, 201). This was certainly colored by his Zionist antipathy to anything having to do with Diaspora life. As the Jews were stateless for well over 1800 years, there could be little doubt in his mind but that they had lost their self-governing skills. The establishment of a state in and of itself was not proof that the Jewish people were ready for managing their own political affairs. This ability would have to be nurtured by the State itself, a sort of political guardianship for a politically adolescent public. The inherent paradox here obviously did not occur to, and certainly didn't bother, Ben-Gurion: how does one autocratically teach one's child to stand on its own two feet?

Finally, there was undoubtedly a degree of self-interest in the matter as well. Once the State came into being, it was clear that the resources at its disposal would soon far surpass those of the party, however dominant Mapai happened to be. As it was inconceivable that the Labor camp would relinquish the reins of power in the foreseeable future (despite some potential diminution of political support; see below), there was little risk involved in such a transfer of power from party to State, and much political benefit to be accrued to the Labor camp's leaders, who also happened to run the government.

Indeed, the real advantage was not necessarily in the amount of *added* power being shifted from the socialist parties to the socialist government. After all, this was merely juggling the same balls by the same juggler from one hand to the other. Rather, it was the *other* (non-socialist) parties' *loss* of control and power that would be the main benefit from Ben-Gurion's perspective. By removing certain functions from *all* the political parties (even his own), his hand could only be strengthened.

Moreover, by the early 1950s it was becoming clear that although the *edot ha'mizrakh* immigrants were by and large going to be part of the blue-collar class in Israel, many of them would not identify with secular socialism as expounded by the Labor camp. While they would probably support the Histadrut for economic reasons, their political vote for left-leaning parties on national issues was far more uncertain. Labor's proportional party support, therefore, was bound to decrease over time. Transfer of authority from party to state was mere prudence in the face of such a possibility.

On the other hand, it was obvious that the fast-growing government white-collar sector of clerks, managers, and other functionaries (increasingly manned by the new immigrants) also would not readily identify with Labor values. *Mamlakhtiut*, however, could provide a meaningful value system for them, thus tying them politically and ideationally to the ruling party.

Mamlakhtiut, then, may have been perceived by the Israeli public as a meaningless shift of power from one political source to another, but in reality it only further concentrated power in the State of Israel's central government, thereby creating the basis for deeper—and certainly more comprehensive—political paternalism. Once again, Ben-Gurion was quite clear on this score. Not only would *mamlakhtiut* be henceforth the dominant approach, but he personally would have no qualms about seeking further paternalistic aid from any quarter, especially in those circumstances where Statism alone proved to be insufficient, as Avi-hai (1974, 75) noted of Israel's first prime minister:

> He outlined two major tasks for the Histadrut: the shaping of the image of the state (its social relationships), and undertaking pioneering tasks in the fields of education, the economy, and society, "which cannot be achieved by the force of coercion and law or by the government bureaucracy *alone*" [my emphasis; S. L-W.].... [H]e clearly placed the supreme national interest above the voluntary act of will and conscience.

Ben-Gurion, therefore, was not about to eviscerate the Histadrut's power—it was to continue to function as a tool for the dissemination of governmental largesse across the board. The question was never really one of whether to weaken socialism in the interests of Statism but how best to exploit the former in the more efficient pursuit of the latter.

Paternalism: To What Extent Was it Necessary?

Was such a general paternalistic approach inevitable? While it may have been partly necessary due to the difficult circumstances of the pre- and early-State periods, the *extent* to which it was applied seems to have gone beyond any real nation building need. Moreover, the Labor movement itself had an early sterling example of nonpaternalistic political life—the kibbutz. To be sure, differences of scale do not enable us to make facile comparisons between the minipolis of the kibbutz and the megapolis of the *yishuv*. Yet certainly some of the kibbutz's highly democratic decisionmaking processes could have been adapted and applied to the larger Jewish society.

More interesting is a related question: was the highly centralized and paternalistic approach in line with Jewish political experience?

Here the answer is decidely negative, and provides the first clue why it was almost inevitable that Israeli centralized governmental paternalism could not last.

In a sense, Ben-Gurion had it all wrong. For one, the use of the word *mamlakhtiut* instead of the equally reasonable *medina'ut* constitutes a strong indication that he was consciously misreading early Jewish political history (Cohen 1987, 202). Whereas *medinah* was far the more prevalent term in the Bible (cited fifty times, by his own account), its general meaning was of a province, large capital, or state, and not an all-encompassing nation or country. Thus, his semineologistic use of *mamlakha* (the larger and more powerful "kingdom"), described merely his own idiosyncratic conception of the State of Israel—despite its being an unnatural type of political construct by Jewish historical standards.

Nor was his mistake a matter only of the first half of Jewish history when the Children of Israel were (usually) sovereign rulers of the Holy Land. Even throughout eighteen hundred years of Diaspora history, the Jewish people managed to develop a very rich and variegated tradition of self-rule. The reason that Ben-Gurion did not see this is that (once more) he viewed the matter from the perspective of national sovereignty, which the Jews did not have in Exile. From the standpoint of political autonomy, as manifested in the Jewish *kehilla* (local community), the Jews had very wide and deep experience in self-governance—at times (due to the peculiar nature of the general feudal system), far greater than their gentile compatriots (Elazar 1981, 23–63). Even more to the point, such governance was highly democratic in nature, with actual elections usually held every year or so.

Nor was such low-level Jewish self-rule merely a function of Diaspora existence. In point of fact, the *kehilla* structure was the real embodiment of Jewish government from time immemorial (thus *medinah*, not *mamlakha*). The Jewish people began their national history as a conglomeration of twelve tribes, each with its own flag, family structure, and (according to legend) specific professional occupation. The first recorded era of Jewish national life took place under a *confederal* political arrangement (Judges, I–XXI), with most legal and political matters taken care of within the tribal structure. Only in national emergencies is an occasional politico-military front formed to resolve the specific problem, and even then of only a few tribes (Judges 7: 35).

An even better indication of where the Jewish political-institutional bent lay was the ensuing monarchical period, when an attempt was made to centralize power in the hands of the king (and let it not be forgotten that even the establishment of the monarchy was literally a

product of grassroots pressure on the prophet Samuel). The arrangement lasted through a mere three monarchs, with civil war erupting
after Solomon's death. Israel would never again be fully united.

What of paternalism from the standpoint of government services? While it would be highly anachronistic (and unfair) to measure
the Bible's social welfare ethic in terms of modern socialism or even
contemporary social democracy, two things do stand out clearly in
the Bible.

First, there is a great amount of concern for social justice, equity,
fair treatment of the poor and downtrodden, etc. From this standpoint, Labor Zionism was but biblical ethicism in modern garb. Second, and more to our point, almost none of these "social welfare" services (except judicial fairness, etc.) were to be directly provided for by
the governing authorities but rather by the general population. There
is no governmental philanthropy in the Bible, merely the insistence
that Jews set aside money and/or agricultural produce (charity in our
terms) for the less fortunate. Even in areas of life which are universally accepted as the exclusive prerogative of the state, e.g. military con-
scription, personal freedom was not completely negated. A coward or
a bridegroom could not be forced into serving (Deut. 20: 8; 24: 5).

What of the later Diaspora period? Didn't we note above that
the Jewish *kehilla* during the long *galut* period had in fact a comprehensive approach to government service provision? The answer is
yes, but this only highlights the hypocrisy of Labor's own approach
(assuming that it consciously copied the *kehilla* model). For the fact of
the matter is that modern Zionism stood for the negation of the Diaspora. Conversely, time and again the Zionist leaders would hark back
to the biblical, pre-Diaspora period, as the only one worthy of providing any sort of model for the renascent Jewish State. Thus, conceptual
consistency should have dictated that the Labor Zionist movement
incorporate the relatively non-Statist principles of the earlier Jewish
Commonwealths in its contemporary system of governance, and not
the governmental values of the Jewish *kehillot*, which it publicly
loathed.

Altogether, then, in its concern for social justice, the public's welfare, etc., it can be said that Labor Zionism's heart was certainly in the
right place from a historical Jewish perspective (i.e., biblical values),
but its hands—the overly centralized institutional means and hyper-
paternalistic political approach—were not in keeping with that earlier
Jewish political culture and tradition. This is not to say that that biblical politico-cultural predilection could by itself roll back the
entrenched paternalistic Israeli system (see Table 1.1), especially given

the political tradition that evolved in the Diaspora communities. Only when it became clear much later that such a system of governance was no longer appropriate and had indeed become bankrupt (literally and figuratively), did the establishment begin tottering and prove to be vulnerable to grassroots demands for a change in governing style and substance. We now turn in the following chapter to the growing manifestations of internal Labor party and general governmental decay, which paved the way for the eventual grassroots revolt.

TABLE 1:

Israeli Governmental Paternalism, Socialism, and
Centralism in Selected Areas of Life

A) Economy
   1- Approximately 25% of the national workforce are employed by government ministries or government corporations (chapter 5).
   2- An additional 18% are employed by the Histadrut and/or its sundry corporations (chapter 1).
   3- 90% of Israeli real estate is owned by the State Lands Authority, which will not sell land but only offer 50-year leases.
   4- The Israeli public is forbidden to carry foreign currency in its possession, prohibited from having foreign currency accounts overseas, and severely limited in the amount of foreign currency that can be removed for overseas trips.
   5- For nonsalaried workers, tax assessments are set by the tax authority based on what it feels the worker's income should be, rather than on what the worker declares it to be. The burden of proof here is legally on the worker.
   6- Due to a system of "golden shares," the vast majority of corporate stockholders have had no say in the management of their companies; management or the original owners maintained full operating control (chapter 5).
   7- Of the country's five major banks, two were party-affiliated, and one more was controlled by the Jewish Agency (chapter 2).
   8- Very high tariffs have been established against many foreign products to "protect" local industries, sometimes for decades without change (chapter 5).
   9- The government set and controlled virtually the entire credit market, as a result of its voracious debt appetite and through sundry bureaucratic and statutory regulations regarding bank lending and pension fund investment (chapter 5).
   10- At times (nonwar years), Israeli government expenditures (central and local authorities, plus other national institutions directly tied to the State) have *exceeded* the *total* gross national product (GNP) (the income generated from all sources). Just the expenditures of the central government alone have

Continued on next page

TABLE 1 *Continued*

reached as high as 76% of GNP — far in excess of any other Western country (chapter 5).

B) Society

1- Matters of personal status — marriage, divorce, conversion — are wholly the province of the Orthodox Rabbinate (chapter 9).

2- Establishment of new settlements is done exclusively by government fiat (chapter 4); numerous new townships were set up in areas of "national need" but not popular demand, to be populated by poor new immigrants with no other choice offered them (chapter 1).

3- No private schools have been established on the elementary level, although an ultra-Orthodox (*Agudat Yisrael*) "independent" system is allowed to exist (chapter 8).

4- Until 1990 there was but one government-controlled TV station, and three government-controlled radio stations. No private stations (even cable) were permitted by law (chapter 6).

5- Half the country's daily newspapers are organs of specific political parties. Every newspaper must have an editor-in-chief over twenty-five years old, who speaks the language of the paper, and possesses no criminal record; two copies of each paper must be delivered daily to the district commissioner; plus other press conditions which remain on the books from the time of the British Mandate.

6- 85% of Israel's population were covered by the Histadrut's *Kupat Cholim* (health system), which did not allow any choice in the patients' selection of a physician (chapter 7).

7- Child adoption is exclusively in the hands of the Social Welfare Ministry, with agency and private adoptions outlawed.

8- A system of monthly government payments exists to encourage an increased number of births.

9- A government-appointed Movie and Theater Censorship Board (the latter abolished in 1991) has decided which productions would not be shown in Israel as they might give offense (political, religious, and/or moral) to various sectors of the public.

C) Polity

1- Local government is financially and administratively beholden to the Interior Ministry (chapter 1).

2- There is no written constitution guaranteeing civil rights, although some "Basic Laws" have been passed by the Knesset over the years regarding government institutions, e.g. presidency, army, Knesset, etc. (chapter 10).

3- Despite its origins under the British Mandate, the Israeli court system has no trial by peers (jury system), but rather exclusively by magistrate.

4- All outdoor protest assemblies of over fifty people must get a police

Continued on next page

TABLE 1 *Continued*

license in order to demonstrate; the police will then set the conditions of the protest (duration, location, etc.).

5- In most of the major parties, candidates for inclusion in their respective Knesset lists were selected until the late 1970s by the upper party leadership (through what was called a *va'adat minuyim*), and rubber stamped by the party's Central Committee (chapter 12).

Note: All of the items in this table were in evidence from 1948 to at least the early Seventies. As will be explained in the course of the book, some of these elements were abolished or reformed in the late seventies and throughout the eighties under the impact of public pressure.

2

Rotting Timbers:
The Decay of the Establishment

Labor Strife

From the outside, the dominant Labor coalition with Mapai in the lead seemed omnipotent in its internal unity and broadbased electoral support. True, there were occasional contretemps between Mapai on the one hand and Mapam or Ahdut Ha'avodah on the other, and even the "Old Man" resigned the prime ministership once in a fit of pique, but overall the image was of monolithic and invincible dominance. Herut's Menachem Begin and his "demagogic" diatribes notwithstanding, the Labor fortress was all but impregnable from without.

But not from within. The very shift from class to nation (Cohen 1987), from partisan socialism to national *mamlakhtiut*, was one source of potential trouble. The interests of Mapai as the standardbearer of the latter ineluctably began to move it away from the interests of the Histadrut, ever loyal to the former. Tensions, not to mention economic work stoppages and occasional general strikes against government policy, increased. The facade of socialist unity was beginning to crack.

This was politically important not only because with declining electoral power the Labor establishment would find it increasingly hard to maintain its hammerlock on the entire social welfare and paternalistic economic system. Equally as crucial for our purposes was the psychological change occurring among the Israeli public as a result of the perceived weakness and increasing fallibility of their formerly omniscient government mentors. As time wore on, and as the establishment bore signs of unmistakeable weakness and disarray, the Israeli public became emboldened to take matters into its own hands, undercutting several of the heretofore "accepted" paternalistic policies of its government.

Electorally, already during the country's second decade small signs began to appear that Labor would not be preeminent forever.

Despite its grip on power and the huge patronage at its disposal, Mapai (and in the 1960s with its allies on a joint list—the small, and later large, Labor Alignment) found it increasingly difficult to maintain its proportional Knesset strength. From a broader perspective, and most germane from our socialist/paternalist standpoint, the entire Left of the party spectrum was starting to lose strength by the mid sixties onwards.

These electoral patterns, however, are easier to pick up in historical hindsight than at the time. More obvious to the contemporary Israeli back then were some highly visible and controversial episodes which expedited Labor's decline in a number of ways.

Most serious, because it was so publicly rancorous, was what came to be known as the Lavon Affair, which erupted and continued to reverberate ever louder in 1960 and 1961. This episode—over the question of who was responsible for an intelligence mishap in the mid fifties—was essentially an internal party affair, and ostensibly had no ideological or cross-party ramifications. Precisely because it was purely internal, and most significantly ended with Ben-Gurion being rebuffed by his own party, the Lavon Affair was important. It proved to be not only enervating from an intraparty standpoint but highly corrosive of the public's trust in what was formerly perceived as a founding party rocksolid in its organizational unity.

The final nail in this particular coffin was Ben-Gurion's defection from the party and "treasonous" creation of a new one: RAFI (Israel Labor List). This was not so much a political precedent (after all, Israeli parties had suffered from the "mitosis syndrome" from even before the State's establishment) but a psychological one of monumental proportions. For if the "founding father" of Israel could leave the very party which he founded, what was to stop mere longtime supporters from doing likewise?

Thus, Mapai and Achdut Ha'avodah dropped from 44.2 percent of the national vote in 1959 (before the Lavon Affair began making a splash) to 41.3 percent in 1961, and declined further to 36.7 percent in 1965 after Ben-Gurion had left the establishment.

Indeed, even had the cataclysmic split not occurred, Ben-Gurion's inevitable leaving the national political scene would by itself have removed a strong psychological impediment to continued public kowtowing to the powers-that-be. This was especially true for the late *yishuv* generation which grew up with Ben-Gurion as the all-knowing political paterfamilias. Could George Washington's compatriots disobey his will or turn their backs on his life's work? Not until he had at least left the scene.

Much the same could be said of the more recent *edot ha'mizrakh* immigrants, albeit from a somewhat different perspective. While not having grown up with the "Old Man," these Jews brought with them from their former autocratic Arab countries a political culture which respected, perhaps even demanded, great political strength from their leaders (Shamir & Arian 1983, 102–105). Such an authoritarian political culture was most receptive to governmental paternalism, especially if delivered by a perceived "real leader." With Ben-Gurion's passing from the scene, the authoritative source of strict political obedience was now removed—paving the way for greater psychological freedom of choice electorally as well as sociopolitically.

It didn't help matters, of course, that Ben-Gurion's Labor successors were not the sort of people to inspire awe and respect among the masses seeking strong and decisive leadership. Levi Eshkol, while highly competent by all accounts, was an extremely colorless leader (this was Weber's "routinization of charisma" with a vengeance!). His disastrous radio talk to the people on the eve of the Six-Day War only reinforced the general impression that an indecisive grandfather, and not a strong founding-father type of leader, was leading the country to war.

Eshkol's successor—Golda Meir—was arguably an improvement on the charisma front, but suffered in some traditional minds from a fatal "flaw": she was a woman! Dynamic maternalism was still not the same thing as forceful paternalism in the eyes of many who had been brought up in a patriarchal culture (this was true as well for numerous Israelis of *ashkenazic* origin). Finally, cerebral Yitzchak Rabin, although a former army chief of staff, proved to be extremely colorless and weak in his aborted three-year stint as prime minister. In short, Labor provided its charges with three problematic leaders in a row, none of whom would come close to inspiring the respectful awe so necessary in maintaining a top-to-bottom political and socioeconomic governing relationship.

If lackluster leadership was a necessary condition for the public's declining willingness to bear political paternalism, it was not sufficient by itself. As suggested above, there would have to be a concomitant change in that public's politico-cultural mentality. Here, ironically, the paternalistic campaign to "modernize" the new immigrants in the fifties proved to be a thorn in Labor's side precisely because it ultimately largely succeeded. By socializing those immigrants into the norms of democracy, by undercutting their previous "subject" political culture, the socialist establishment made it easier for them to attack the "system" and abandon the very party which brought them to their Promised Land. As we shall witness in the next chapter, uncoincidentally it was the children of the earlier immigrants—educated in democratic Israel, but somehow not benefitting from the paternalistic system—who began the massive waves of public protests, which constituted the first sign that the Israeli grassroots revolt had arrived. Labor was thus hoist with its own petard.

"May'avdut Le'herut": Freedom From Labor's Dominance

Coincidentally and simultaneously, the opposition was laying the groundwork for a viable ideological and electoral alternative. Herut, led by firebrand Menachem Begin, was never at a loss for sniping at Labor, but his image was too much the maverick to be supported by any but the most disenchanted of Israelis. The alliance between that outcast party and the very genteel Liberal party in 1965 (the alliance was then called Gahal, to be changed in 1973 to Likud with the addition of three other small parties) lent a great amount of legitimacy to the previously politically ostracized Revisionists.

Further reinforcing this trend was the National Unity government set up in 1967, incorporating Gahal in practice into the halls of power. No longer could the Labor establishment claim that Mapai & Co. was the only viable governing alternative on the Israeli political scene. By the late sixties the Israeli public had not only witnessed the spectacle of Labor disunity, but even more incredibly the granting of an official imprimatur to its archrival.

Were this series of events merely a slow political changing of the guard, it would have had little relevance to the more fundamental issue of governmental paternalism. But the battle between Labor and the Likud—especially before the territories issue became so salient in the 1980s (after the Egypt peace treaty established a precedent for territorial withdrawal)—was much greater than that, extending into the socioeconomic ideological realm as well. Legitimizing the Likud meant that its quasi-laissez faire philosophy was now something that could at least be considered in rational discourse—whether on the plane of public policy or private action. The belief that the government *should* provide so much for so many, was henceforth no longer an automatic given for increasing numbers of Likud supporters.

From where did the Likud's basic electoral support come? In the 1920s and 1930s most of the voters for Jabotinsky's Revisionist party had arrived in the Fourth Aliyah (during the late twenties) from Poland, with petit bourgeois and professional backgrounds. Their obvious economic interests were not to be found in the socialist camp, but their aggressive nationalism would not make them feel comfortable among the Liberals or Progressives either (the latter finding heavy support among the Germans fleeing Hitler in the Fifth Aliyah).

In the seventies, a somewhat surprising antipathy to socialism and paternalism began to emerge on the other side of the political fence. While obviously not influenced by the Likud's platform, growing numbers of traditional Labor voters began to entertain thoughts of electoral defection. Here, once again, it was Labor's success which paved the way for its own ideological and public policy demise. How so?

As a fundamentally materialistic doctrine, socialism (even of the Zionist stripe) in principle never stood against an increase in national or private wealth. Only wealth gained by exploitation of one's fellow was opprobrious. In any case, the Labor establishment—helped by massive foreign aid from world Jewry, as well as even larger amounts of German reparations money—had succeeded by the seventies in creating quite a broad middle class, precisely from the formerly proletarian stratum that formed the core of its political support.

For these nouveau bourgeois, Labor's continuing policy of heavyhanded governmental direction and economic interventionism began to look increasingly unappetizing. As a result of rising education and disposable income, Israel's broad middle class was becoming increasingly restive with a system that continued to treat them as social and economic adolescents. The question, of course, is why the Labor party did not heed this increasingly obvious groundswell demanding greater freedom of action.

A number of factors were at play, and an in-depth analysis of them all would lead us too far astray here. The central elements in this miscommunication were as follows:

1) The party system was in the midst of a serious process of organizational atrophy, thereby divorcing the Labor leaders from their changing constituency (Lehman-Wilzig 1990b, 92–98).

2) The ongoing close relationship between the Labor party and the Histadrut made it extremely difficult to change course ideologically. As noted above, their respective supporters were becoming increasingly differentiated in their interests, but the institutional links were too strong and complex to be easily or painlessly disconnected. Even as late as 1990, an internal suggestion for disassociating the two monoliths met with stinging rebuke from party leader Peres and Histadrut general-secretary Kessar (*Jerusalem Post*, 9/28/90, 2).

3) Labor continued to harbor the hope that the new Israeli proletariat—the *edot ha'mizrakh*—would halt their defections to the Likud

and return to the bosom of socialism out of pure economic self-interest. It was almost impossible to expect that Labor Zionists could conceive of nationalism becoming more salient an issue than economics. The (vain) hope was that any loss of middle class supporters would be more than offset by the inclusion of the new *edot ha'mizrakh* voters, the children of the 1950s' immigrants who had been taken care of by Mapai.

Such was not to be the case. Not only had nationalism become more important an issue for this major population sector, but their recollection (or conception, for those too young to actually remember) of the earlier absorption process was not too complimentary to Labor. Worse still, the fact that as a group the *edot ha'mizrakh* still had lower socioeconomic status in the seventies, was viewed by this once proud community as being the conscious—and discriminatory—fault of the Labor establishment. As a result, for many *edot ha'mizrakh* their objective need for government paternalism conflicted with the subjective loathing they held for the governmental provider of those services. It was not so much the *act* of providing which initially turned them off; rather, the hated *source* of such paternalistic welfare proved to be the death knell of such a public policy philosophy.

Nor was this merely a matter of subjective perception. The increasingly visible and (for Israel) shocking revelations of government financial malfeasance provided Labor's opponents with more than enough objective ammunition against the "system" as it had developed. No matter that such scandals were not really the "fault" of overcentralization and paternalism, but rather the expression of Acton's aphorism that "power corrupts, and absolute power corrupts absolutely." Between Asher Yadlin's massive transferral of public funds to party coffers and Yitzchak Rabin's wife's technical misdemeanor of not closing her foreign currency account in Washington, the general feeling was that the country's socialist leadership was ethically inferior to the common man in the street. There was no longer any moral force behind the government directing society in such a comprehensive fashion.

The same held true on the cognitive plane as well. True, the Lavon Affair hinted at the fact that the country's leadership was not infallible, but the issue involved was so abstruse and remote from the public's daily life that in the final analysis the whole controversy had little visceral impact. The same could certainly not be said for the *mekhdal* (debacle) of the 1973 Yom Kippur War.

Here was an issue of life and death, and the authorities had blown it. Adding insult to injury, the mudslinging and counteraccusations among the various levels and departments was unseemly to say the least, especially as the beloved and highly respected army high command was put in the dock by the politicians attempting to cover their political backsides. The Agranat Commission's findings, which cleared the political side of direct culpability to the detriment of the army, did not help matters; indeed, they may have even further eroded the government's moral standing as a result of its perceived spinelessness in passing the buck.

In any event, by the time the dust had cleared in the aftermath of the Yom Kippur War, no one in Israel could still maintain the intellectual superiority of the leaders over their ostensible political charges. From now on the government would be hard put to rule by fiat without convincing the public of the wisdom and necessity of its policy. Such a situation was not very conducive to the continuance of blindly accepted government paternalism.

Still, both the Lavon Affair and even the *mekhdal* were seeming examples of individual human fallibility (the latter, of course, comprising many more people). An argument could still be made that they did not reflect on the entire system but rather on certain purveyors of that system. It was not really until the eighties that the full bankruptcy of the system became clear for all to see—and this despite the fact that it was now the Likud which was running the show.

After the "Mahapakh": The End(lessness) of Paternalism

Before describing the economic debacles of the 1980s, which constituted the final nail in Israel's centralized/paternalistic coffin, it would be worthwhile to stop for a moment and analyze why the Likud did not immediately dismantle the entire system upon its accession to power in 1977. For the grassroots revolt which constitutes the central subject of this book—while facilitated and expedited in great measure by Likud ideology, as has already been briefly noted—occurred in large part during that party's tenure in office and took little account of the change in political party preeminence.

The classic Likud argument was that it failed in dismantling the socialist paternalistic system because of the conscious sabotage of the still regnant Labor establishment. Given the fact that the bureaucracy was overwhelmingly supportive of Labor's way of doing things (even if not all such government workers actually voted for the Left parties in the elections)—after all, that was their life's work—a single Likud election victory (or even two) was hardly enough to force a radical break with the accretions of the past twenty-nine (or more) years. Much the same argument was advanced by Richard Nixon in the face

of an "intransigent" New Deal federal bureaucracy. This is certainly
not the place to assess the relative veracity of such a claim. Suffice it
to say that despite its logic, there were several other factors involved
here as we are about to see.

To begin with, almost all of Prime Minister Begin's entire efforts
were concentrated on foreign policy, by choice and as a result of the
radical changes in Egyptian-Israeli relations soon after his accession
to power in 1977. However, he understood little of economics per se
and had never exhibited any interest in such matters. To the contrary,
on two separate historic occasions he discounted the benefits of massive economic aid because of higher principle and national pride:
fighting against accepting German reparations in the early fifties, and
summarily dismissing America's offer of a large grant in compensa-
tion for withdrawing from military bases in the Sinai. True, this set a
good precedent for national economic nondependence on foreign
sources, but it also illustrated his serious lack of understanding of
macroeconomics.

Who then was in charge of economics during the Likud reign,
and what was the government's official economic policy? While the
Likud ostensibly had a liberal/laissez faire philosophy, this was
mostly true of the Liberal party wing within the Likud. For better or
for worse, however, that party faction had increasingly become the
junior partner in the alliance over the years, with far less internal
power than the Herut party. When push came to shove within the
overall Likud, it was usually the broader electoral interests of the
party that tended to carry the day.

Which leads to the next important aspect of the question. From
the time that Menachem Begin had taken over the leadership role in
Herut (after the more intellectual Jabotinsky had passed away in
1940), a strong populistic strain began to emerge in that party. This
was greatly reinforced by the continuing addition of hundreds of
thousands of lower class (especially *edot ha'mizrakh*) supporters who
ultimately brought the Likud to power. It was clear to the party that
this group should not be antagonized through any significant reduction in social welfare services. With the meteoric rise of David Levy
(who represented this constituency) as a key power broker within the
party, any such reduction in governmental economic paternalism
would have been most forcefully resisted within Herut itself.

To be sure, there was no official talk of dreaded socialism, but in
practice—other than some liberalization of foreign currency restrictions and minor tax reductions—the Likud carried out much the same
policy as had Labor! Moreover, in light of its Knesset elections suc-

cess, the Likud hoped ultimately to be victorious in the Histadrut elections as well (even putting up Levy as candidate for general secretary) and, therefore, did little which might antagonize the still needy working class.

Thus, it was no coincidence that elements of the Israeli welfare state system began to be dismantled only after both major parties joined together in 1984, thereby providing mutual sustenance and cover from the remaining populist-socialists in their respective midst. Indeed, the hyperinflation of the Likud years, which was caused by overexpansion of the money supply, could be viewed as a peculiar form of liberal paternalism—spoiling the children by affording them a spending spree of monumental proportions. Likud economic policy, therefore, combined the worst of both worlds: unearned government largesse freely bestowed upon the public, coupled with no significant contraction of Israel's traditional social welfare network.

The ensuing economic debacle forced the Unity government's hand in the latter part of the eighties, commencing the era of belt tightening and governmental fiscal retrenchment. As we shall see in part II of the book, by then the public was way ahead of the authorities in their undermining of the entire paternalistic system. It was not a matter of the government finally "seeing the light" but rather of it trying to react to the downfall of the entire apparatus as a result of decay from within, and attacks from without.

In short, if the increasing ossification of the system under the Labor party's hegemony was a *sufficient* condition for the grassroots revolt, the subsequent continuation of such a general public policy approach on the part of the Likud once it came into power rendered such a revolt *necessary*. As long as a potential political alternative existed to the paternalistic/socialistic establishment, public dissatisfaction was felt on the political plane through such means as widespread public protest, which at least promised to speed the eventual downfall of the ruling party. When that indeed did occur in the late seventies (a change of the political guard, i.e., the *mahapakh*), but still no significant socioeconomic public policy change was forthcoming, there was little left for the Israeli middle class to do but take matters into its own hands. It left the formal system entirely to its own devices, while establishing alternative and/or complementary socioeconomic "networks," which might provide the public with what it wanted.

Thus, it was the very victory of the Likud in the electoral sphere, coupled with its subsequent failure to translate that victory into concrete changes, that galvanized the public into initiating its grassroots revolts in so many issue areas. With both political camps having proved themselves unable to change the system, the public obviously decided to go it alone.

Countergovernment: Alternative Public Models

This is not to say that certain elements within the governing system did not see the handwriting on the wall earlier and attempt to protect themselves through the establishment of complementary institutions, which would enable them to function in adequate fashion. Indeed, these governmental examples can even be said to have served as role models for the public's circumvention of the official system, in concept if not actual application.

The most notable example of such an alternative/complementary institution was the Jerusalem Foundation established by the mayor of Israel's capital city, Teddy Kollek (subsequently copied by Tel Aviv and other Israeli municipalities). Such an organization—highly distinctive (and probably unique in the world) in that it is independent of the Jewish Agency, World Zionist Organization, and the Finance Ministry—collects funds from overseas donors in order to pay for municipal projects that the regular authorities (local or national) cannot, or will not, finance themselves.

This was not a minor factor on the Jerusalem political scene—the Jerusalem Foundation's income and disbursements accounted for a *sixth* of the entire operating municipal budget by 1980 (Sharkansky 1987, 11). Even more germane is the fact that none of the conventional mechanisms of political accountability are in play here; it is a situation where elected officials use independent resources for public activities in order to be free of the restrictions and guidelines of their political "superiors" in the national ministries.

More amorphous, but far more widespread, is the behavior of many officials working within Israel's public administration. Whether such an approach to governance has been on the increase in the past two decades is a matter of some debate, but there is little doubt that the public has come to increasingly recognize (and subsequntly mimic) such a behavioral proclivity among those within the system:

Despite the heavy weight of formal procedures that are centralized in government ministries, it is befitting the inhabitants of the Jewish state that they behave as entrepreneurs within their public sector, sometimes ignoring or evading the laws that they have enacted against themselves. Also, they are willing to pursue policy goals indirectly when circumstances deter a direct pursuit of their goals. Officials break the formal rules frequently. Sometimes they break the informal rules as well. It can be difficult sorting out the violations that are permitted in the interest of flexibility, and the violations that are condemned as corruption (Sharkansky 1987, 2).

Thus, from the seventies onwards the Israeli public had clear models of circumventional behavior emanating from precisely the last place one would normally expect to find them—the political and bureaucratic establishment itself! As long as the overall system was perceived to be at least adequately fulfilling its mandate (as was the case by and large through the early seventies), the citizenry felt little need to apply the lessons from above to their own public behavior. With the increasingly obvious dysfunctioning of the government, though, the Israeli public did not have far to look in order to come up with ideas as to how to perform their own "bypass operations." The model was there for all to see and replicate adaptively.

The Bankruptcy of Economic Big Brotherhood

When did it become it patently clear that the authorities had lost their grip on things? What exactly occurred to the system in the eighties that constituted a knockout punch to the philosophy and practice of socialistic paternalism? We shall be detailing several of the subsidiary phenomena in part II, in their respective chapters. For now, it should suffice to broadly highlight the key events of that domestically tumultuous decade.

The hyperinflation which took off at an 111 percent per annum inflation rate in 1979, reached its zenith in the summer of 1985 with inflation near the end running at close to an annual rate of 800 percent! Overall, from 1978 to 1984 consumer prices increased by well over *20,000 percent* on an accumulated basis (Sharkansky 1987, 63).

The effects of that hyperinflation were socially corrosive to say the least. From a personal psychological perspective, Israelis spent an inordinate amount of time worrying and acting to keep ahead of the financial treadmill—running to the bank daily to shift savings from one vehicle to another; purchasing the latest goods before prices rose yet again. From a sociopsychological standpoint hyperinflation was no less problematic because it pushed the public into an "every man for himself" mode of thought in a sinking economy. Indeed, this merely reinforced and further aggravated the already nascent self-help mentality of the Israeli public. With the economic system no longer functioning as it was supposed to, Israelis began to think and behave in terms of seeking and applying novel, noninstitutional, personal solutions to what was really a collective problem. This was "grassroots" personified in spirit, if not in its less than constructive outcome.

During the first part of this period, the only ones who seemed to be concerned were the economists (except for Israel's first-ever finance minister with an educational background in economics— Yoram Aridor) because the general population lived in a fool's paradise of easy money. This was most true of the stock market, as prices rose on a daily basis for a number of *years* due to the banks "guaranteeing" ever higher prices for their own shares, through supporting and manipulating their own stocks. Here was economic paternalism of the first order from two sectors: the government bribing the public with monetary goodies; the banks with surefire profits.

The collapse of the stock market in 1983 devastated the economy. In the short-term, that catastrophe actually increased the level of governmental economic intervention as it had no choice but to bail out Israel's four largest banks, which were caught with huge amounts of worthless stock collateral and debts far in excess of any potential future profits. Virtual nationalization of the banking system ensued, with the government henceforth the nominal owner of almost all the country's major banking institutitons (only in 1990 was it able to begin the process of bank privatization in order to relieve itself of the burden)—but at an astronomical loss of a couple of billion dollars!

Here, too, the psychological cost to the public was no less damaging. This time the Israelis were hit where it hurt the most—in their pockets—and the ensuing distrust of governmental advice and policy was profound. One interesting thing which fueled the public's disgruntlement was the fact that during this period the government's overall budget outlay increased in real terms, but almost all of this increase went into higher levels of debt servicing, with most ministries suffering from declines or at best stagnation in the funds available to them (Sharkansky 1987, 73). The public was thus hit twice over: it saw the government getting (and spending) more money, but it was being provided with fewer services! Such a situation was not designed to heighten confidence in the official service system and certainly was an added factor paving the way to the public's decision to "go it alone."

By the mid eighties, total deterioration had set in. The public's outrage and frustration was replaced by fear as inflation continued to skyrocket, threatening to tear apart the fabric of society (the economic cloth was long since tattered). Strong measures were called for in this real crisis.

Perestroika in the Holy Land

The result was paradoxical in its own way. On the one hand, the public turned to the government and virtually demanded that it do something to rectify the situation. This was a reversion to the kind of paternalistic mentality that had been ebbing for some time. On the other hand, what the government did—indeed, the only thing it could have done to get Israel out of the quagmire—was to begin to take apart the paternalistic/socialist economic system which had been in place for decades. This was inevitable, because the government had to stop overprinting money and so was forced to cut back on the largesse and handouts, which the public had come to expect as their natural right.

Subsidies for basic commodities were slashed; grants to encourage an increase in the birthrate were diminished; the civil service workforce was reduced. Most astonishing of all (especially for the unfortunate Israelis involved), the government for the first time in its history refused to channel money to ailing firms in order to save workers from the unemployment lines.

The success of the 1985 New Economic Program (NEP, the third such-named program since 1977), did not have the effect of restoring public confidence in the government's omniscience. Indeed, it was public knowledge that this program was a product of academic consultants called in to devise it, free from the intervention of the politicians with their political considerations and machinations. It certainly did reinforce the public's conviction (as if it needed much more convincing after the economic debacle of the early eighties) that the less governmental involvement in their lives, the better.

As a consequence, and also in response to the grassroots revolts, which became more and more widespread over time (as we shall see in the coming chapters), the government began to embark on a far-reaching program of further liberalization and privatization in the latter part of the decade. The stock market was reformed to allow the shareholders greater power and say in the management of their companies. The authorities—no longer fearful of losing full control of the national economy (which doesn't exist in any case anywhere in the contemporary democratic world)—began to encourage foreign purchase of Israeli companies as well as relatively unrestricted access of Israelis to foreign loans.

Most significantly, a large-scale program of privatization of government corporations was started, with an initial goal of selling off approximately $7 billion worth of State holdings (above and beyond the quasi-nationalized banks). With the announcement in late 1989 of the willingness to sell off El Al (Israel's national airline), a profound change was obviously in the wings for traditional Israeli economic paternalism. The successful sale to the public in late 1990 of shares in Bezek, Israel's telephone company, was further proof that a dramatic shift in macro-economic relations had indeed taken place (*Jerusalem Post* 9/26/90, 6).

Red is Dead: The Decline of the Histadrut

Where was the Histadrut during this period of socialist regression, and why wasn't it in the forefront of a vigorous attempt to stem the capitalist tide? The answer lies in the simple fact that Israel's giant trade federation was undergoing much the same economic trauma as the rest of the country, and thus was in no position to find fault with the government's macroeconomic policy when its own management of the Histadrut empire was failing badly.

We shall return to several specific instances of Histadrut problems in some forthcoming chapters so that we need here merely to paint the broad outlines of its travails. Its huge construction company Solel Boneh was the first to be hit hard by the New Economic Policy of contraction of government spending, and the Histadrut found itself in the very embarassing position of having to fire a few thousand of its own construction workers. Worse was yet to come; soon the gigantic conglomerate Koor began to undergo serious financial strains in 1988, culminating in technical bankruptcy a year later due to its inability to pay off overseas creditors. Only the forceful intervention of the government (bridging loans, pressure on local bank creditors, etc.) enabled it to stay afloat. Nevertheless, by late 1990 it is still unclear whether this central pillar of Histadrut economic power will continue to exist at all, much less in its traditonal form.

Overall, then, the Histadrut found itself increasingly beholden to government largesse at precisely the time in Israel's history that such a policy was becoming increasingly unpopular with the public, not to mention the growing unwillingness and inability of the government to continue the practice of corporate dole, which had been *de rigeuer* in the past. Any sustained Histadrut attack on the general new economic policy would have redounded to the detriment—and possibly the death knell—of the Histadrut as one of the country's largest corporate owners and employers and, overall, as a central pillar of the national economy.

On the other hand, while the traditional Histadrut Labor establishment did manage to fend off the Likud in the November 1989 elections, it was not clear beforehand that such a victory was assured. In order not to alienate many of its supporters who voted for the Likud in the national Knesset elections, even on the trade union side the Histadrut Laborites restrained themselves from being too belligerent against the highly popular Likud finance minister (Nissim) during the 1986–88 period.

In short, the government's only potential major opponent found itself with both hands tied (as employer, as well as representative of the employees), leaving little in the way of real political or economic resistance to the nation's policy of retrenchment from socialism and economic paternalism.

The Israeli Phenomenon in World Context

If much of this latter program sounds very similar to the Reagan/Thatcher revolution, that too is no coincidence. Israel had long looked to the United States (and to a lesser, but still palpable, extent to its former Mandatory master Great Britain) as a primary political, cultural, and especially economic role model. The significant changes occurring in those two countries could not but influence Israeli policy as well, although typically about a decade late.

Thus, the massive American anti-Vietnam War and Civil Rights protest movements of the sixties were replicated exactly in Israel in the seventies with the social riots of 1971 and the postwar protests in 1974 (although here not emanating from the campuses). Even the name Black Panthers was copied by the slum dwellers of Musrara from their counterparts in Watts! The 1980s merely shifted the role modeling from the sociopolitical to the economic sphere.

That the New Economic Policy occurred at the same historical juncture as the rise of Michael Gorbachev to power and the beginning of Communist *perestroika* is not altogether coincidental either. To be sure, there was nothing necessarily fated about their both happening in 1985 (nor did the world fully realize what was about to occur in the Eastern Bloc). On the other hand, several global forces were ineluctably driving almost all the world's socialist countries in the opposite direction: increased economic trade and competition, rising expectations of their populations as a result of the international media, etc. The State of Israel, especially sensitive and vulnerable to world economic trends, could not help but go along sooner or later. We shall return to this cross-comparative theme in the book's final chapter.

In one sense, then, Israel's grassroots revolt was not completely indigenous. Many of its tactics were learned from overseas sources (although quite a number of new wrinkles have been added by the Israelis), and the philosophy underlying such a social uprising was certainly not original to Israel. This is not to say that the whole phenomenon is merely a gigantic mimicking of overseas trends. As we have seen in this chapter, the increasingly obvious and disastrous flaws and distortions of Israeli paternalism merely meant that external events would be able to find an open Israeli ear.

In the final analysis, Israel's grassroots revolt was not historically original in the world, but this is not to suggest that it has been merely derivative. On the contrary, it evolved in large part out of a distinctly local felt need and real objective circumstances. The public's move to circumvent and undermine the increasingly stifling paternalistic system in Israel (and not only in the economic realm) was socially spontaneous, if not altogether novel by international standards in its basic conception (again, see chapter 14). Nevertheless, given the depth and breadth of such paternalism in Israel (with all its shortcomings), the revolt would of necessity take on certain characteristics in some specific areas of life not to be found in any other country undergoing "de-paternalization."

3

Brushfires: Early Grassroots Awakenings

First Awakenings

It was no coincidence that the first manifestations of public discontent and concomitant muscle flexing appeared in the political arena because that was the essential source of the establishment's power and paternalism. It was only after the initial baptism of grassroots fire in extraparliamentary activity during the seventies that the stage was set for the more widespread socioeconomic extrainstitutional behavior in the eighties. The latter was but an extension and expansion of the former as we shall see in the coming chapters. In this chapter, though, we shall explore not only the evolution of grassroots political pressure but the reasons for the public's complementing its direct protest approach with the more indirect undermining of the system in the social and economic arenas.

This is not to say that no semblance of grassroots discontent existed prior to the 1970s. In fact, almost immediately upon the establishment of the State of Israel, relatively serious social turmoil emerged in the "temporary" camps among the new immigrants from the Arab world. The multitudinous reasons for that outbreak need not concern us here (Lehman-Wilzig 1990b, 29–34), but already at that stage one could perceive the beginnings of public intolerance for heavy-handed governmental interference in the lives of the new citizens.

As noted in the first chapter, the Labor establishment from the start decided to embark upon a policy of modernization and acculturation of the *edot ha'mizrakh* into the norms of modern society. Such a decision was made, of course, without consultation with those communities' leaders, and notwithstanding the significant trauma that the latter had already suffered in the very act of uprooting themselves from their native countries to come to their alien homeland. Among other things, the immigrants' traditional religious practices came under intense attack and proved to be the first spark in their violent reaction. Thus, for instance, the camp authorities forcibly sheared off beards and sidelocks (of adults and children alike), disingenuously arguing that it was a hygienic step to prevent the spread of lice; children were given material incentives to attend secular schools; some evidence even suggests that several hundred *edot ha'mizrakh* children were "kidnapped" from hospitals and surreptitiously given over to secular *ashkenazi* families for private adoption (Levitan 1983, 254–291). The response to all these paternalistic practices was not long in coming, as riots against the authorities occurred in several of the camps.

Nevertheless, this was a transitory phenomenon and not at all indicative of any aversion to paternalism with a human face. Far more frequent during this early period—both inside and outside the camps—were vociferous (and occasionally violent) demonstrations demanding that the government supply "Bread and Work." The government, of course, did not view such demands as being intrinsically unacceptable; quite the reverse, there was universal agreement in Israel that indeed it was the government's role to look out for its charges and aid them as much as possible. The specific problem at the time was merely the inadequate resources in Israel for meeting all those needs.

In short, not every street eruption in the first two decades of Israel's existence could be viewed as nascent antipaternalism or a move away from socialism. The public, no less than the government, agreed that in most areas of life the authorities were required to service, and act on behalf of, their constituents. Only truly outrageous interventionism would elicit a strong public response during this early period, and after a while the authorities usually came to respect the dividing line between obligatory paternalism and impermissible meddling.

Grassrooting for the Underdogs

The first major break in the Israeli public's fifteen-year docility actually emerged from a group demanding *more*, and not less, government intervention—the Black Panthers (Cohen 1972, 93–110; Cromer 1976, 403–413). These were the second generation *edot ha'mizrakh* who were still stuck in the Jerusalem slum neighborhoods, with little hope for their future. In "spontaneous" riots and demonstrations in 1971—there are indications that they were coached by some social welfare workers (Cromer 1976, 409)—the Black Panthers demanded greater assistance in ameliorating their impoverished condition.

This set off a wave of other protesting groups on a host of issues. The "Young Couples" not only demonstrated in the street for weeks and months for more housing credits, but they started a new (and ultimately widely used) tactic of "creating facts" in the field. In fairly large groups, they began squatting in new, but still not tenanted, public housing projects to try and force the government's hand (Etzioni-Halevy 1975, 502–504).

In one sense, of course, philosophically both these groups were still on the side of greater government involvement. However, their nontraditional behavior only served to highlight an increasingly obvious fact—it was precisely the very system of socialist paternalism that was failing to get the Black Panthers out of the slums and had not succeeded in creating sufficient housing for the country's young adults. By taking matters into their own hands, these (and other) groups were displaying in the public arena rare (for Israel at that time) personal initiative and were pointing the way to a completely different philosophy, which would soon envelop their compatriots.

The galvanizing effect of the Black Panthers on the rest of Israeli society was stunning (Lehman-Wilzig 1990b, 37–44). Whereas the period of 1955–1970 was marked by less than forty protest events annually on average, the 1971–1978 years averaged more than 120 protest events (the 1979–1986 period, for which somewhat exact data are available, was marked by more than two hundred such events per year)! The slumbering giant in the Israeli "street" was awakening with a vengeance.

The Center Breaks Loose

If the Black Panthers constituted a grassroots revolt on the periphery of Israeli society, the post-Yom Kippur War demonstrations marked the modern emergence of mainstream Israel's grassroots pressure. It started modestly enough: in early 1974, a solitary reserve officer, Motti Ashkenazi, took it upon himself to protest in front of the prime minister's office against the mishandling of the situation in the days prior to, and immediately after, the outbreak of the war. This soon mushroomed into massive public protests, which led to the rapid downfall of the Golda Meir government.

The significance was twofold. First, it highlighted in the starkest terms possible just how weak the Labor establishment had become if it could be felled in just two months of public pressure (and this almost immediately after that government had legitimately won its seats in democratic elections held in late 1973). The internal party decay discussed in chapter 2 was now patent for all to see. Second, this protest wave and its successful conclusion constituted the first

real and publicly obvious lesson of "people power" in the Israeli context. In short, not only was the emperor shown to have little clothes
left, but his subjects learned that they, too, could actually change the
governmental wardrobe.

Nor was this the end of that specific story. The postwar protest
movement spawned a new political party—Shinui (Change)—which
eventually joined with an even larger grassroots political organization
led by a former chief of staff and renowned archaeologist, Yigal
Yadin. This umbrella party, called DASH (the Hebrew acronym for
the Democratic Movement for Change), was the first Israeli party to
institute a system of primaries to select its Knesset candidates—an
obvious slap at the highly centralized approach of *all* of Israel's large
parties.

Even more important than this was the party's platform. For the
first time in Israeli history a major party spent the majority of its
rhetorical and electoral energies in an attempt to change what had
heretofore been perceived as the "technicalities" of the Israeli system
of government. In other words, instead of concentrating only on the
"big" issues of war and peace, economic prosperity, etc., this neo-
phyte party consciously emphasized systemic issues that it felt needed to be addressed. This was a high-risk approach, especially in a
"hot-blooded" country such as Israel. For who would possibly be
interested in such "dry" issues as electoral reform, even with "clean
government" as an additional come-on?

The results proved otherwise. DASH won an incredible fifteen
seats in its first Knesset run in 1977, drawing away enough voters
from Labor to give the Likud its first-ever national election victory.
Indeed, as the election results (and subsequent analysis) made clear,
this was far less a rousing victory for the Likud than a strong rebuke
of Labor and its policies. It wasn't so much that the Israeli public had
completely identified with ultranationalism and capitalistic laissez
faire but rather that it was no longer willing to accept the overbearing
application of Labor socialism and paternalism. In that sense, the voting public did not exactly get what it wanted—a coalition between
Labor and DASH, with the latter forcing radical change of the former—but instead got the Likud, a real alternative to Labor philosophy and policy (at least in theory).

Be that as it may, on the morn of May 18, 1977 all Israelis arose in
shock and wonderment at what they had wrought. The seemingly
invincible Labor coalition had fallen (none of the pollsters and pundits
had predicted that the Likud would emerge victorious), and the common man had accomplished this major upheaval through the ballot

box. This was not precisely a grassroots revolt in an extraparliamentary sense, and had matters followed their "normal" course, such a revolt might have died out as a result of the new government's implementation of real structural reform. Unfortunately, such was not to be.

Political Revolt and its Aftermath

The immediate and specific evidence that the formal/electoral approach was insufficient for the public's purposes was the rather rapid disintegration and demise of DASH. Perhaps it was too democratic, or perhaps it shouldn't have joined the Likud's right-wing government coalition. Whatever the reason, this experiment in using electoral means to reform the system proved to be an abject failure.

Worse yet, and far broader in its ramifications, was the fact that the Likud did little to change the paternalistic approach of governance or even (demagogic pronouncements notwithstanding) to abolish most of the country's more egregious socialist policies. The reasons for this were already discussed in the previous chapter, but in light of the hopes which arose subsequent to the Likud's rise to power, its inability or unwillingness to change matters in any significant fashion proved to be a mortal blow to public confidence in the system's ability to reform itself. There no longer existed much enthusiasm or continued will on the part of the public to pursue its grassroots revolt through electoral and/or parliamentary channels (the only surviving vestige of the DASH debacle was the original Shinui party, which managed to garner a maximum three seats through the 1980s). The public's energies over most of the ensuing decade henceforth turned to beating the system, rather than changing it.

Resources and Resourcefulness

Overall, then, the decade of the seventies provided the sufficient conditions for the subsequent large-scale grassroots revolt: flawed economic policies, inability of the Likud to significantly change the socialist system, and (as we have just seen) the equal inability of the public to reform the political system through electoral, legislative, and even "routine" extraparliamentary means. One necessary condition was still lacking until the eighties: enough private economic resources in the hands of the public to enable the citizens to financially maintain alternative systems of public services. In other words, the existence of a grassroots desire to circumvent the system had to be accompanied by the ability to do so.

Paradoxically, it was only during the late 1970s and early 1980s that enough Israeli citizens had reached the stage of middle class financial security, if not outright wealth. Why paradoxically? Because the steady improvement in many Israelis' personal economic situation occurred simultaneous to the national economic condition going from bad to worse.

There is no contradiction here. Part of this microimprovement came at the expense of the macroeconomy. For example (further elaborated upon in chapter 5), income tax evasion and illegal foreign currency transactions reached very high levels in the eighties—enriching a segment of the public while impoverishing the national treasury. Indeed, one might speculate (there is no proof for this) that this very gap between perceived private wealth and public poverty merely reinforced in the minds of many Israelis the idea that they understood economics better than the government did!

In any case, by the 1980s this burgeoning middle class had money to spare "under the mattress"—and in the bank, for Israelis consistently have had among the highest personal savings rates in the world. In the 1965–1989 period, the private savings rate ranged from 20 percent to 38 percent (Bank of Israel 1990, 31), as compared to about 5 percent in the United States, for instance. This essentially enabled them to seek out and pay for alternative services, as we shall see in the coming chapters: afternoon classes for their children, private health care, pirate cable television, etc.

Another important resource should be added here: higher education. A new generation was coming of age in Israel and for the first time a significant number of its leading members had gone through college (the universities were by then conferring over 15,000 bachelor's degrees a year). The social self-assurance and self-reliance of this generation was quite patently beyond that of the previous generations; these younger and more well-educated Israelis had no qualms—and enough requisite knowledge and savvy—to try and "go it alone" in the rubble of failed government policy and services.

The combination of better economic standing and higher educational attainments also explains in part the almost complete lack of governmental willingness to seriously attack the grassroots revolt, even in its illegal manifestations. The reason for this unwillingness is obvious, for no longer were the authorities dealing with unsophisticated lower class people but rather a powerful middle class, which constituted the central electoral battleground between the Labor party and the Likud. Neither side wished to antagonize this large group through "overzealous" prosecution of the laws. To be sure, this did not mean that everything was permissible. For instance, once it became obvious that the pirate cable television phenomenon had come under the control of Israeli "organized crime" (in Israel, still almost exclusively lower class), the authorities began prosecuting the perpetrators more assiduously. Significantly, however, there was never any thought of prosecuting the subscribers to illegal cable television; the electoral damage would have been too great.

In sum, the authorities were caught between the anvil and the hammer. The public's ability to sustain its revolt was now quite high while the government's willingness (and capability) to battle it was rather low. In such a situation where the resource gap was actually widening over time, there was little to stem the grassroots tide. We turn now to the second section of the book in which the full strength and scope of this phenomenon is described and analyzed.

Part II

Issues

4

National Security: Settling Scores

Holy Land Grab

Virtually all the protest movements discussed in the previous chapter (with the occasional exception of the Young Couples) had at least one thing in common: their protests, whatever the specific issue and through whichever type of demonstration, were geared almost exclusively to bringing pressure to bear on the political leaders so that the governing authorities themselves would change policy, alter direction, and/or reform the formal apparatus. There was little thought among these protesters of actually accomplishing anything through the establishment of a *fait accompli* in the field.

The importance of this should not be underestimated. As long as such extraparliamentary activity had as its goal mere accepted and normal political pressure, such movements in a sense had not yet completely weaned themselves from the paternalistic conception that the government was the only possible (or legitimate) engine for carrying out change. In other words, while such earlier movements had taken the important psychological step of challenging public policy or the government's general approach, this still did not constitute the ultimate step of believing that they had the right or the ability to go it alone.

That step was first taken by Gush Emunim (Bloc of the Faithful)—the young guard of the mainstream Zionist National Religious party (NRP). This internal party faction/movement evolved out of Israel's territorial conquests of the 1967 Six-Day War, and it held to the messianically unshakeable belief that Judea and Samaria (the West Bank) was part and parcel of the biblical Land of Israel and therefore the State of Israel as well (Ra'anan 1981).

The Labor governments, while not about to quickly relinquish those territories without a bona fide peace treaty with Jordan (and even under such an hypothetical and ideal circumstance Labor was split), was also in no great hurry to allow Jewish settlement in an area brimming with a rather large local Arab population (numbering about

800,000 souls). It was into this policy vacuum that Gush Emunim stepped with a grassroots forcefulness not seen heretofore in Israel.

The strategy was relatively simple in and of itself, but behind it lay layers of political and symbolic complexity which made this issue a marvelous first step in the door for the grassroots revolt which was about to engulf the country. After prolonged political pressure within their own party and against the broader Labor coalition (of which the NRP was a member at that time), the members of Gush Emunim in the mid seventies began to establish "settlements" in the territories through well-planned overnight forays. By the time the sun would rise in the morning, several families were already living in temporary shelters with the Israeli flag waving defiantly over their settlement.

True, technically the first instance of such private settlement occurred in Hebron in April 1968 when Rabbi Moshe Levinger and some supporters leased the Park Hotel in the center of town, ostensibly to celebrate Passover in the city of the patriarchs—and then refused to leave. However, the resolution then was the establishment by the government of a town (Kiryat Arba) outside of Hebron (Efrat 1988, 60–63), so that the public perception was not necessarily of any "victory" for Levinger & Co. In any case, there was no followup to this for several years, and the media eventually left the story alone, so that the overall impact was minimal. Quite the reverse was the case with Sebastia and subsequent overnight settlement forays in the mid seventies, with increasing public attention and controversy accompanying the Gush Emunim campaign.

At first the army, at the behest of the civilian government, forcibly removed the Gush settlers only to have the experience repeated soon thereafter. After a number of such attempts, the government hit upon a compromise solution at Sebastia in the Samarian hills: the group of settlers would be ensconced in an "army base," and eventually that base would be removed but not the civilian settlers. Notwithstanding the legal and public relations fiction, it was apparent that the strategy of "going it alone" had worked, setting a precedent for many more such citizen-initiated settlements thereafter.

Why had the government given in, and why was this the perfect issue for getting the grassroots revolt rolling? To begin with, Gush Emunim understood that it was not standing alone in this struggle against official government policy, and that the Labor party would be hard put to permanently stop the settlers. This was due to the fragile coalition of the Rabin administration, dependent as it was on the NRP—not to mention the existence of a split between settlement hawks and doves internally within the Labor party itself. If the Labor establishment had been suffering from increasing enervation in general, its weakness was especially obvious on this particular issue.

Beyond this, however, lay an ideological/symbolic element of tremendous import. Zionism had always been associated in the minds of the pioneering public with a couple of activities, which really constituted two sides of the same Zionist coin: *aliyah* (immigration to Israel) and *hit'yashvut* (settlement of the land). Especially in an era of declining Zionist ideology (not just of the socialist variety), it was very difficult for any Zionist party—let alone the one which traditionally was in the forefront of such *hit'yashvut*—to call a halt to a younger generation willing to sacrifice for the ideal of "settling the land," merely because the latter hadn't yet received the authorities' official sanction. Ben-Gurion's generation had not exactly asked the Ottomans or the British for permission to settle the Holy Land; could his successors easily stand in the way of those who were merely following in the early pioneers' metaphorical footsteps?

The government's (understandable) failure to put its foot down and dictate policy set a precedent not only on the specific issue of settling the territories but, as time would prove, on all significant issues of public policy where a minority had strong feelings or interests. Once the precedent had been set, it became exceedingly difficult to turn back the tide.

This is not to say that it did not try on several occasions to quash such quasi-private political initiative, especially on the settlement issue. Such governmental reactions were to be expected, of course, not only because of the diplomatic and strategic sensitivity of the whole subject but also due to the fact that for an Israeli establishment so used to directing the national show it was very difficult to accept the possibility of any other actor in the lead determining actual public policy.

In the end, however, such governmental efforts only made matters worse—even when it won significant victories on this front. For, the greater the struggle between the government and Gush Emunim, the more media coverage it engendered and the more Israeli citizens began to grapple with the concept (at least in principle) of working at cross-purposes to official policy. This was true even among those population groups sympathetic to the government's attempts to limit West Bank settlement; the occasional much-ballyhooed successes of Gush Emunim began to give other groups some ideas regarding their own general approach.

The public situation on this score became even more confused with the rise of the Likud to power, for now a certain ideological and moral legitimacy was lent groups such as Gush Emunim. The latter, a protest and oppositionist political action group par excellence, was almost the mirror image of the Likud, Israel's "perpetual" opposition. The fact that the Likud in power found it hard to shed its oppositionist rhetoric and political style, reinforced all the more Gush Emunim's increasing public legitimacy.

The settlement grassroots revolt reached its zenith in early 1982 with Israel's withdrawal from Sinai in general, and the new city of Yamit specifically, as a result of the peace treaty with Egypt. Gush Emunim, along with other right-wing groups, formed the "Stop the Withdrawal from Sinai" protest movement and, once again, became involved not merely in verbal protesting but in a physical attempt to maintain and perpetuate the settlement of that area. The denouement was an actual "fight" against the army (Aran, 1985).

The Limits of Political Revolt

The government's victory in this specific episode is instructive from a number of different standpoints, with an important lesson regarding the grassroots phenomenon in general. To begin with, here at least the country's rulers had the overwhelming support of the Israeli public for their policy. This meant that Israel's authorities—in their overall handling, or nonhandling, of the sundry deviant groups throughout the 1980s—took account of the political environment in which each respective struggle was being carried out.

Significantly, in the vast majority of the issue areas, which will be outlined in the coming chapters, one finds that a majority of the public is involved in (or at least support) the "revolting" group. In other words, these grassroots revolts were not really antidemocratic but rather "only" antinormative (in the sense of transgressing the official law at the time). Each revolt marked the expression of the majority will, frustrated in the course of regular democratic procedure. When a majority (or at least a large minority) was not behind a specific grassroots revolt—as was the case in Yamit—it tended to fail.

The second point here, connected to the first, is that Israel's grassroots revolts are *not* a threat to the existence of the democratic regime (see chapter 12). Even the mere hint of potential regime destabilization was enough to lose the "Stop the Withdrawal" movement whatever sympathy it may have had originally among the Israeli public. Given the international repercussions of Israel's reneging on the Egyptian peace treaty's provisions, the Israeli public would not countenance even the possibility of a loss of national face. Clearly, after having waited almost two thousand years for their own sovereign country, the Jews of Israel will not at this stage do anything which might threaten its fundamental stability.

This has been especially true of the extreme right. Given their supernationalism, it has been especially difficult for them to consider endangering the fragile State despite some profound disagreements with those who may be running the government at any specific moment. The first serious conflict of this sort essentially set the stage for all that was to come: the Altalena Affair. Menachem Begin's refusal to hand over all the arms on that ship to the State's army in 1948 led to its sinking at the order of Prime Minister Ben-Gurion. This was as close to civil war as the Jewish State had ever come, but Begin stepped back from the brink, extremely reluctant to jeopardize the ultimate prize of Jewish national sovereignty so recently won. Future right-wing extremism would also stop at the ultimate act of rebellion, notwithstanding several attempts at disobedience and low-level revolt.

Thus, the participants in the entire grassroots phenomenon have walked a fine, but clearly identifiable, line: undermining and circum-venting governmental social and economic policy is acceptable, but nothing shall be allowed to threaten the foundations of the democrat-ic system qua system. Once again, this is a rather widespread revolt against the flaws of the governmental structure and its output; it is not a revolution bent on the system's downfall.

A more recent proof of this could be found in the ultimate act of revolt emanating from a small group from within Gush Emunim—what came to be called the Jewish Underground. This assemblage of about twenty-five Jewish settlers/terrorists (the correct type of appel-lation was itself a matter of some controversy) conspired and suc-ceeded in attacking, maiming, and killing several Arab West Bank mayors and officials, plus other innocent Arab civilians, in reprisal for Arab terrorist attacks on Jewish settlers.

Once the Israeli authorities uncovered this underground, it pro-ceeded quite forthrightly in prosecuting the members involved. The public, too, stood overwhelmingly against their actions (in a country where it is exceedingly difficult to find a pro-Arab majority on any issue). The reason was clear. Despite numerous rhetorical justifications for the Jewish Underground's deeds, it was obvious that here the road was perilously close to the Hobbesian abyss. Any grassroots action seemingly supplanting the army's role was considered well beyond the pale of social revolt. The Jewish Underground had crossed the fine line mentioned above by a substantial margin, and both the authorities and the public at large would not countenance even so much as a precedent being set on this slippery revolutionary slope.

This was illustrated again most recently in the authorities' handling of a group of settlers which had begun to organize towards the establishment of the Nation of Judah in Judea and Samaria in the eventuality of Israeli withdrawal from the territories. The press (*Ha'aretz* 5/26/89, 5a) reported on a full panoply of national regalia—flag, constitution, etc.—and the authorities' response was not long in coming: interrogations and arrests of the suspected protorevolutionaries (*Ha'aretz* 7/30/89, 3; 1/12/90, 3). That the organizers were not prosecuted in the end due to a narrow reading of the law by the attorney general, is somewhat beside the point (*Ha'aretz* 4/29/90a, 2), although it may be reflective of at least some minimal support among the general Israeli population, and probably even more (tacit and active) support among the settlement communities in the territories (*Ha'aretz* 1/26/90, 7).

Are there continued manifestations of more widespread right-wing grassroots activities in the territories? The answer is affirmative, and they most exquisitely delineate the gray area between the permissible and impermissible, which was noted previously. The topic? Settler vigilantism (Weisburd 1989).

Due to the occasional danger of travel in the West Bank, the IDF has permitted settlers to carry weapons with them as a matter of due course. The problems begin to arise when the use of those weapons seems to go beyond the bounds of the necessary or prudent. This is true not only in the almost daily occurrences of a settler shooting at Palestinian youth throwing rocks from a distance, but especially in the more infrequent (but not rare) instances where whole groups of settlers rampage through Arab villages, smashing windshields, and destroying property, in reprisal for earlier attacks on one of their own.

Here is an incendiary problem from a number of perspectives. On the one hand, the authorities cannot (and usually do not) allow such group vigilante campaigns to go uninvestigated, and some perpetrators are occasionally brought to trial (especially if they are high-profile leaders such as Daniella Weiss—the former secretary-general of Gush Emunim—or Rabbi Moshe Levinger of Hebron fame). The army cannot be perceived as relinquishing its sole authority of maintaining order in the territories, and so it must at least offer the public perception (some would say illusion) that it is on top of things and will not countenance such violent grassroots behavior.

On the other hand, the IDF cannot possibly guard every settler, every road, and every hill. There does in fact exist an objective personal security problem that cannot be ignored. Therefore, the matter on many occasions boils down to a question of semantics: is it "vigilante action" or is it simple self-defense?

Making the issue even more complicated in Israeli eyes is the existence within Israel proper of *mishmar ezrakhi*, the officially sanctioned quasi-civilian local guard. If those Israelis can move around the cities with weapons defending the citizenry, why shouldn't the settlers be able to, living as they do in a far more hostile environment?

Thus, the general public is of two minds on the issue of settler grassroots vigilantism, for such activity is potentially threatening to the sole authority of the IDF, but it is also seen as being necessary on occasion. The authorities too are somewhat torn—not wishing to present any theoretical opening for real "private initiative" in the realm of security but also recognizing its own limitations in this regard. At best, Israeli society as a whole has learned to live with such an uncomfortable (and not always manageable) ambivalent approach. At worst, however, it does tend to offer the impression that grassroots activity—even on so sensitive an issue as national security—has at least a modicum of justification. Still, the line has not been unalterably blurred.

None of this is to say that Gush Emunim has abandoned its original grassroots activity—settlement. As the nineties dawned with the opening of the floodgates in the Soviet Union, the State of Israel found itself with the "problem" of absorbing tens of thousands Russian Jewish immigrants virtually overnight. Notwithstanding the domestic and international brouhaha over settling a large number in the territories, Gush Emunim immediately put into action a plan to settle two thousand immigrant families within the territories through its own investment in temporary structures (*Ha'aretz* 1/26/90, 2). Such an independent grassroots program, while presenting a direct threat once again to government control in this highly sensitive area, could not be easily stymied for reasons noted earlier: it combined two of the most sacrosanct Zionist values in one—*aliyah* and *hit'yashvut*. Once again, the government found itself following, rather than leading, its activist public.

Pressure from the Left

When we turn to the left of the political spectrum, we find that the overall grassroots position of the public is similar on the national security issue. On the one hand, the alter ego protest movement to Gush Emunim—Peace Now—enjoys no less widespread public support (and usually manages to outdraw the right in its protest size). Peace Now never did get involved in any physical challenges against government policy (a la forcibly removing West Bank settlements). Thus, it has remained throughout a traditional protest movement of burning passion, but less than incendiary activity (Bar-On 1985).

The same cannot be said of other, much smaller, groups on Israel's dovish left. For instance, *Yesh G'vul* ("There is a Limit") is a movement that began in protest against Israel's 1982 War in Lebanon (officially called "Operation Peace for Galilee") but more recently has turned its attention to the occupied territories. Its tactic, too, is physical in a pacifistic sort of way: encouraging conscientious objection on the part of army recruits and reservists to refuse to serve in the territories.

Conscientious objection, of course, is hardly original to Israel. What is unusual, however, is the rather minimal level of public support this grassroots tactic has garnered. When compared to the proportional levels of conscientious objection found in America during the Vietnam War, the phenomenon in Israel is slight. In the three years of Israel's occupation of Southern Lebanon a mere 140 Israeli soldiers (mainly reservists) refused to serve (Wolffsohn 1987, 95–96). During the more troubled *intifada* (Palestinian uprising) years 1988–89, approximately only 150 cases of refusal to serve (for reasons of conscience) were recorded, and many of them were multiple refusals by the same soldiers.

On the face of it, these low levels are somewhat surprising given the general Israeli tendency to protest, and especially in light of the large number of Israelis with serious misgivings regarding Israeli policy in the territories. Why, then, the weakness of this particular grassroots revolt? Once again, because it potentially could threaten the very existence of the State of Israel. Any threat to the functioning of the IDF is perceived by the Israeli public as undermining the nation's foundations, given the parlous state of its security situation. Here, too, "revolt" is tantamount to potential revolution, and the Israeli public—despite some unhappiness with the government's handling of the situation in the West Bank and Gaza (especially after the outbreak of the *intifada*)—will not support even principled actions against the security authorities. Nevertheless, as shall be explained in chapter 11, there is no guarantee that this situation will last forever, and there may even be some additional elements emerging more recently that could enlarge the scope of this phenomenon on the Israeli scene.

An even clearer expression of Israeli society's lack of willingness at present to undermine the country's security can be seen in the public's reaction to what by all democratic lights should have sent thousands of civil libertarians into the streets, if not storming the barricades. With the continuation of the Likud's hold on power (even after it had to share the seat of government with Labor from 1984 until 1990), a few Israelis in positions of some influence—whether journalists or political functionaries—began to carry the principle of do-it-yourself into the realm of foreign policy. The favorite ploy was to attend an international conference where it was known that representatives of the Palestine Liberation Organization (PLO) would be in attendance, and conduct talks with them in the hope of "bringing the two sides closer together."

Whatever one may think of such an unusual public/private improvisational approach, the Israeli government's response was to pass a law making it illegal to even talk with members of the PLO or any other terrorist organization—anywhere in the world! This was not only an abridgement of free speech but an overzealous expansion of territorial jurisdiction. Nevertheless, in 1989 Abie Nathan—the popular Israeli radio personality, philanthropist, and peace seeker (he had flown a private plane from Israel to Nasser's Egypt in 1968 to advance the cause of peace, much to both sides' consternation)—was indicted, convicted, and sentenced to six months in jail on the basis of this new law. The public's reaction? Strangely muted, almost silent.

True, Nathan's friends came to his defense and the media were skeptical about any damage he may have done to national security, but there was little grassroots outcry in favor of this universally liked (if not always agreed with) personality. The reason, once again, was the "limit of revolt," which constitutes an unwritten norm of contemporary Israeli society. There must be an area in which the government continues to rule almost supreme (at least until the next election), otherwise anarchy—or even worse, strategic politico-military weakness—ensues. Undermining the army or the foreign policy apparatus is beyond the red line in Israeli terms.

In the final analysis, Israel's grassroots revolts are not only homegrown affairs (as they must be, otherwise they wouldn't be truly grassroots), but they must also stay close to home. Forcing the creation of new settlements over the Green Line (Israel's internationally recognized pre-1967 border) is about the maximum grassroots action that will be tolerated in the national security area—by most of the general public and the governing authorities. Still, the fact that even in this sensitive realm some sort of independent grassroots activity was countenanced and not resisted strongly by the government was an indication of what lay ahead in less dangerous areas of Israeli life.

5

Economy: Blue and Black

Governmental Dominance

Israel is a singular country in a number of different areas of life. When it comes to economics, however, the situation here is altogether unique—from a number of perspectives. While chapter one explained at length the general factors underlying Israel's unusual economic development, i.e. the reasons behind its heavy emphasis on paternalism, centralism, and especially socialism, it would be useful at this stage to statistically delineate some of the more egregious aspects of Israel's "economics" before venturing on a discussion of the public's grassroots response to such a system.

The most readily understandable (and internationally comparable) economic figure which suggests the extent of government involvement in a country's life is its budgetary outlay (other indicators will be discussed later on in this chapter). The International Monetary Fund (IMF) reported that for 1980 Israel was the clear winner among all Western democracies in this category with government expenditures amounting to 76 percent of the country's gross domestic product, as compared to runners-up Ireland and Sweden far behind at 51 percent and 41 percent respectively (IMF, 1983). The 1990 estimate is of approximately the same ratio (75 percent): total government expenditures of 62.5 billion shekels out of a gross national product (GNP) projected at about 84 billion shekels (Rabushka 1990b, 25)!

Even that, however, understates the magnitude of the involvement: Israel's own Central Bureau of Statistics takes into account a wider net of governmental services, e.g. spending by the government, local authorities, and national institutions under the government's control (but receiving funds from abroad). During the Likud's first five years in office these expenditures reached the level of 95 percent to 105 percent of the GNP (i.e. of all income received by the authorities)! Put simply, Israel's entire governmental apparatus has on occasion (during nonwar years, no less) spent more than all the money the entire country has been able to generate from within and without (Sharkansky, 1987:24)!

Such extragovernmental components of Israel's trade and commerce are critical to understanding the breadth of governmental involvement and intervention in the country's economy. And let it be noted here at the outset that the main factor behind such heavy outlays and involvement is not national security and defense: during the period 1960–1986 nondefense outlays have grown twice as fast as defense-related expenditures (Rabushka & Hanke 1989, 15).

How was the government's control and involvement in the economy manifested? Again in 1980 (a not unrepresentative year in relation to these data), there were 213 listed government corporations, subsidiaries, and joint ventures, employing 64,000 workers (only 22,000 less than all the official and standard government ministries and agencies combined). And all this does not include the Histadrut, which owned at that time 1,100 firms employing 100,000 workers, with another 1,400 cooperative enterprises associated with it in one form or another, incorporating an additional 170,000 employees (Rabushka & Hanke 1989, 26–27).

By 1990, under the impact of forces to be described shortly, the situation had improved somewhat. Yet there still remained 160 government corporations, employing over 27 percent of the nation's workforce. And despite serious financial difficulties, the Histadrut sector of the economy (25 percent of all companies in the country) continued to employ 18.5 percent of the nation's workers (Rabushka 1990b, 6). Altogether, these governmental and nonprivate economic entities over the years have traditionally employed close to half of Israel's workforce, exerting a major influence on most of the others through their economic and political clout.

One could go on and on: Israel's two largest banks by far (Leumi and Hapoalim), respectively controlled and owned by the World Zionist Organization and the Histadrut; the nation's accumulated foreign debt reaching 125 percent of GNP in 1984, illustrating the extent of dependence on foreign sources of national income (indeed, in 1980 international monetary transfers to Israel amounted to a sixth of GNP); the import/GNP ratio—another measure of national self-insufficiency—generally hovering around 0.70, completely beyond the 0.21 general average for developing countries, not to mention the 0.15 average for developed ones (Rabushka & Hanke 1989, 28).

One additional (incredible) aspect should suffice at this stage, and in fact will explain why the grassroots revolts appeared almost of necessity:

In 1960 Israel's national income per capita stood at 85 percent of the average national income per capita shown by some two dozen Western, developed countries. In 1980 Israel's national income per capita was only 51 percent of the average shown by the same group of Western countries. In the interim, Israel's national income per capita had grown by 180 percent after controlling for inflation. When compared to the greater growth elsewhere in the West, however, Israel's national income per capita had declined by 40 percent (Rabushka & Hanke 1989, 33)!

Put succinctly, despite a very sharp absolute (and real) increase in national income over two decades, Israelis suffered a steep decline in disposable income relative to other Western countries. Indeed, the situation was bleakest in the later period. Whereas real annual GNP growth per capita was a hefty 5.6 percent from 1960–1972, this declined to a paltry 0.4 percent for the 1974–1985 period (Rabushka & Hanke 1989, 2).

What was the cause of all this? The answer is somewhat paradoxical, for the average Israeli's situation was actually much better than these numbers would indicate. Yet this very mitigating factor would prove to be the source of the revolts.

In order to understand this conundrum, a few additional statistics must be offered. From the early sixties until the mid eighties, transfer payments from the government to the public increased in real terms by more than *300 percent:* from 5 percent of GNP to 18 percent! Indeed, government subsidies alone (for basic commodities and credit) went from 2 percent to 13 percent of GNP between 1960 and 1981 (Rabushka & Hanke 1989, 3).

What did this in effect mean? Simply stated, due to the socialist nature of the economy the governing authorities managed to provide public services far in excess of that found elsewhere in the West— "free" of (private) charge. For example, basic food and other commodities were sold at well below real cost; the same held true for transportation, health, and education services, among others. Thus, the Israeli with a comparatively lower income could still afford a decent standard of living, certainly above what one might think based on a superficial glance at the preceding income figures. But the real macro cost was inefficient use of such nationally distributed monies, while the micro price was reduced personal freedom for the citizenry in deciding how best to avail themselves of such necessities. It was the latter especially which fomented the swelling urge to find ways to undermine and circumvent the increasingly paternalistic and constricting economic system.

In what could only be called (in hindsight) the clarion call for the economic grassroots revolt which was about to overwhelm Israel, Milton Friedman delivered the commencement address at Hebrew University on the Fourth of July (!) 1977, a mere month and a half after the political *mahapakh* (revolt) brought the Likud to power for the first time in Israel's history. It was the conflict between the public and the private *weltanschauungen* which formed the core of his analysis, and in essence set the tone of the following decade's events:

> Two Jewish traditions seemed to me at war in Israel: a hundred-year old tradition of belief in paternalistic socialist government and rejection of capitalism and free markets; and a two thousand-year old tradition, developed out of the necessities of the Diaspora, of self-reliance and voluntary cooperation, of ingenuity in getting around government controls, of using every device of Jewish ingenuity to take advantage of such market opportunities as escaped the clumsy grasp of government officials (Kimmerling 1983, 119).

Grassroots Economics

Nowhere was the public's revolt more evident than in the area of foreign currency. In one sense this was ironic as the Likud's declared and implemented policy was to loosen foreign currency restrictions on private citizens. Unfortunately, due to the immediate rise of rampant inflation and its concomitant general air of economic uncertainty and instability, plus the continuing high rates of taxation, the public began to hoard huge amounts of greenbacks under their *balatot* (the standard marbled floor tiles in every apartment). Lilienblum Street in Tel Aviv (the actual sidewalk itself) became the money-changing hub of this illegal, albeit highly public, commerce in Black Dollars. This phenomenon became so widespread and "accepted" that by the early eighties virtually all of Israel's daily newspapers were publishing the Black Dollar rate alongside the official bank rate—on their front page!

The amounts involved are of course hard to come by and assess, but the sum of $5 billion seems to have been the average educated estimate. Just to give one indirect example of the continuing dimensions of the phenomenon, 600,000 Israelis went on an overseas trip in 1989, purchasing $30 million in foreign currency from the banks at the official rate. This, of course, is an absurdly low figure as it works out to a mere $50 a head, when the usual expenditure on a foreign trip is approximately $1,000 per person, conservatively speaking. Thus, something on the order of $570 million in illegal black market dollars (whether purchased from dealers or pulled out from under the floor) were expended in a single year. It can be safely assumed that this one-year outlay (for travel alone; the above figure takes no account of black market domestic expenditures) did not nearly exhaust the financial capabilities of the Israeli public.

It need hardly be stated that even a sum half of $5 billion (in a $25 billion economy) would have severely undermined any government's attempts at fiscal policymaking. Indeed, any governmental contraction of the money supply to bring down inflation would be met with the redemption of dollars into shekels (in order to keep private consumption at the high levels to which the Israeli public had become accustomed), thereby further feeding inflation.

That the public's revolt had carried the day became quite evident in the mid eighties when the media got wind of the Finance Ministry's plan of official "dollarization" of the Israeli economy—putting the Israeli economy on the dollar standard. While this was never carried out due to Zionist sovereignty considerations (under such a program Israeli monetary policy would have been set by the Federal Reserve in Washington), it was an admission that the Israeli street was leading the economic charge, and not the government's economic policymakers. The Finance Minister in office at the time, Yoram Aridor, resigned as a result. He was not the first nor the last (actually the third of four) in the seven-year Likud reign to leave as a result of an inability to control the economic bucking bronco with the public in the saddle.

Where had the seemingly singular dollarization idea come from? The market itself, which had earlier moved to an unofficial dollar standard in most of the big-ticket areas, e.g. housing, cars, and the like (indeed, the government ultimately passed a law making it a crime to quote prices in dollars; the public's response was to advertise the price "in shekels equivalent to the sum of X dollars"). While dollar bills usually did not change hands in such transactions, by pegging the dominant consumer items to the dollar, the greenback became the *de facto* currency of choice for the Israeli populace during the hyperinflationary years. The government's monetary dog, therefore, merely began mimicking the public's wagging financial tail.

The same held true regarding the issue of devaluations. From the establishment of the State, occasional devaluations of the Israeli lira were a necessity in order to maintain the profitability of the country's vital export sector. However, whereas in the first few decades such devaluations occurred once every couple of years and were announced with no prior public inkling, from 1975–1985 the government's policy changed to one of "creeping devaluation" (with an ill-fated one-year attempt in late 1977 to allow the currency to float freely).

A game of monetary cat and mouse ensued, which in one sense became the obverse side of the Black Dollar phenomenon. The Israeli public—increasingly sensitive to the faltering hyperinflationary economy—began to purchase dollars in ever larger amounts (legally through controlled bank accounts), thereby increasing the velocity of the shekel's devaluation (the lira's successor). The winner in this upward spiral was the Israeli public (a good part of the entire population in the late seventies and early eighties), which purchased foreign currency to stay ahead of the devaluations. The consistent loser was the government, which found itself not only unable to erode the public's purchasing power but having to deal with ever higher inflation as a result of the precipitous decline in the national currency.

This is not to say that the public always came out on top; on occasion everyone emerged the loser. Most dramatically, this occurred at the time of Aridor's dollarization leak. The Israeli stock market had been on an incredible roll straight up for several years (way beyond even the hyperinflationary consumer price index), with the public eagerly buying the bank shares, which were "guaranteed" (directly by the banks themselves through price supports, and indirectly by the government interested in mopping up excess consumer purchasing power)—guaranteed to rise in price forever. The dollarization program leak, however, led the highly sophisticated (yet gullible) Israeli investors to dump their shekel stocks in a mad dash for foreign currency cover. The bank shares collapsed and with them the entire market bubble as well, wiping out a couple of billions of dollars in the public's savings (despite, and in part because of, the government's guaranteeing all shareholders a mere 6 percent *total dollar* return for holding their shares from 1983-1989).

In a "normal" market system, such an unmitigated financial debacle would have crippled the economy and led to a deep recession, if not outright depression. In the Israeli case, nothing of the sort happened. Why? The amount of foreign currency held (and sold off) illegally by the public was sufficient to carry the Israelis through this difficult period, providing enough economic stimulus to avert a macro-economic downturn. Indeed, inflation actually reached new heights in 1984—445 percent for the year—hardly a sign of contraction!

The real question, of course, is where did all these Black Dollars come from? As was noted above, the technical answer is Lilienblum

Street and its moneychangers, but that avoids the fundamental source. Here we turn to perhaps the central example of Israeli economic revolt: the underground economy.

Few countries in the world would deign to claim that their economic activity is totally above board and fully taxed. For various reasons (not all of them sinister), a small proportion of every national economy falls between the bureaucratic cracks and beyond the grasp of the tax authorities. However, notwithstanding the methodological difficulties of assessing and comparing the extent of such underground economic activity between nations, there seems to be little doubt that regarding the developed world Israel ranks among the leaders in its underground economy generally, and tax avoidance specifically. One study in the early 1980s placed Israel tied for fifth among twenty nations, with its Black Economy (*kalkalah shekhorah*, as it is called) constituting some 10–15 percent of GNP (Tanzi 1984, 328). Using a somewhat different methodology, another researcher found that by 1977 it had already reached 15 percent of GNP as compared to the approximate averages of 3.5 percent for England, 3.6 percent for Sweden, and 4–10 percent in the United States (Zilberfarb 1984, 320–322).

The major factor behind such large-scale undeclared economic activity is not hard to find: Israel's extremely high income tax rate. At one point it had reached a top bracket of 80 percent, but even the 60 percent rate in force through much of the seventies was obviously considered unduly burdensome by many Israelis. Indeed, income tax is not the whole story, for social security assessments (up to a ceiling more than double the average monthly income) have reached the 16 percent mark for self-employed workers (those with the greatest incentive, and opportunity, to cheat on their taxes). Be that as it may, as a result of this public irresistible force the government's once immovable object of high taxation began to give way again in the late eighties, with the upper tax bracket lowered to 48 percent and promises of further reductions in the offing.

The Power of Popular Inaction

Not all of the Israeli public's economic grassroots revolt manifested itself in specific actions. At times it has been stubborn inaction which forced the authorities' hand. Such was the case in the aftermath of the stock market disaster. No matter what incentives the government tried to offer the public to return to the market, it was of no avail. In 1989, only 5.5 percent of the public's savings were invested in stocks—a number which hadn't changed at all since late 1984

(Rabushka 1990a, 24). Even the ironclad promise of no future capital gains taxation (just about the only important thing in Israel that isn't taxed) has not been enough to lure the public back in any significant fashion. Once burned, twice shy? Not really.

The real problem here lay in one of the more bizarre elements of Israeli paternalism—the golden stock share. If, as mentioned above, Bank Leumi was controlled by the World Zionist Organization, it was not due to any large-scale investment in a sizable block of the bank's shares (*Ma'ariv* 1989, 51). Rather, it had to do with a two-tiered system of stock shares whereby over 99 percent of the shareholders had no voting rights, while the owners of a miniscule proportion controlled the entire operation through their exclusive voting power (usually obtained as a result of the start-up investment; subsequent shares issued to the general public did not come with voting rights). Such an arrangement was the standard one among most of Israel's top firms, enabling management to run their firms with full authority but no market accountability (*Ma'ariv* 6/14/88, 12–13).

Once the market bubble burst in the early eighties, Israeli investors were no longer willing to play a game with such lopsided rules arrayed against them. Their very obvious refusal to become involved in the market once again—even after the economy had stabilized in the late eighties, and share prices began a renewed but moderate rise (due mainly to institutional investment)—constituted a silent and passive revolt of the first order.

Once again, a successful one. The four largest banks had become nationalized in all but name (parenthetically, it was no accident that the fastest growing bank in all of the 1980s was the fifth largest, The First International Bank—the only one which had refused from the start to play the stock support game, and thus managed to increase client confidence and business). As noted above, in order to head off a total economic holocaust, the government promised investors (who held on to their bank shares during the 1983 crisis) a guaranteed return by 1990.

As the latter redemption date approached, however, it became obvious that without a blanket equalization of voting shares the public would continue to stay away from the market in droves, thereby undermining the authorities' sincere efforts to encourage capital investment with which to stimulate growth. Therefore, the comprehensive stock market reform proposal of the late eighties—recommended by a government commission, but still not fully implemented—was less a product of the market's earlier disaster and more a result of the public's refusal to be paternalistically manhandled on the corporate management front.

Concomitantly, the government was also responsible for a related problem which had even greater paternalistic overtones: its total domination of the Israeli credit market. Suffice it to say that given the huge internal and external debt that it had piled up from the mid seventies onwards, plus the highly restrictive laws regarding the kinds of investments which banks, pension funds, and others could make, there was no real private credit market to speak of. As a result, a circumventory "gray credit market" arose with no governmental supervision—ending in disaster on a number of fronts throughout the 1980s: scandals, indictments, and most significantly the economic collapse of many kibbutzim which had gotten themselves involved in seeking such no-strings-attached loans in the heady and hyperinflationary days of the early eighties.

Here too the government began to change policy despite, or more correctly because of, the public's underground investment activity and ensuing credit debacle. Whereas only 31 percent of the country's credit was nongovernmentally "directed" (as the euphemistic phrase goes in Israel), that figure rose to 54 percent in 1989 (Rabushka 1990a, 20). Other technical, but highly liberating, reforms were instituted in mid 1989 (Rabushka 1990a, 24), so that in principle and increasingly in fact the Israeli government is fast moving out of the direct credit control business. The most recent economic reforms of September 1990 which included the right of all Israelis to borrow money from overseas sources, further loosened the governmental reins over the domestic credit market.

Public inaction could also encourage correct government policy when necessary. In other words, on occasion the very lack of broad-based public revolt was a sign that the disappearance of economic paternalism was accepted by Israeli society. This became increasingly clear in the late 1980s under the impact of the 1985 New Economic Policy, which finally brought inflation under relative control.

Two of the key components to this critical program were a major reduction in real private income and the discontinuance of the traditional policy of saving bankrupt companies through government largesse. Many commentators predicted that the country would degenerate into chaotic social turmoil if wages and income were cut by more than a few percent. In 1986, though, while the average net income in the public sector declined, there was no appreciable rise in protest or other antigovernment activity of note (Lehman-Wilzig 1990b, 41)—in large part because real wages in the business sector rose along with industrial output.

Moreover, when the giant ATA Textile firm declared bankrupt-

cy soon after the 1985 NEP came into effect, the country was astound-
ed that the government was willing to allow so many workers to be
unemployed. The real surprise, however, was not the headline-grab-
bing daily demonstrations (some violent) by the ATA workers against
the government's lack of aid, but rather the almost total lack of
demonstrative public support for the plight of the workers and/or
lack of antagonism to the government which was trying to set a very
"unIsraeli" noninterventionist precedent.

These were clear indications that Israel's grassroots revolts,
especially on the economic front, were not a mindless reaction to anything that an increasingly mistrusted and weak government might try
to do. On the political front, Israelis continued to have no compunc-
tions about protesting in large-scale demonstrations against perceived
mistakes; on various social fronts, as can be seen in some of our other
chapters, the grassroots revolts continued to manifest themselves
against continued bad policy. But overall, the revolts here obviously
were by no means of the knee-jerk variety. Even when it became evident that the government's new policy was genuinely and palpably
painful, Israelis began to decrease their "revolting" behavior in favor
of that policy—precisely because it was perceived to be leading ultimately in an antipaternalistic, nonsocialistic direction.

In retrospect, such absence of sustained open opposition to the
government's new get-tough policy should not really have come as
much of a surprise. Already at the start of the decade there were clear
indications of a change in public attitudes. As two Israeli sociologists
discovered in their 1980 survey, the average Israeli by then had
evolved "several attitudes: an almost universal toughness in economic affairs...; a not entirely crystallized resistance to government intervention in the economy and to socialist solutions to socioeconomic
problems; and a decidedly materialist outlook and set of values, par-
ticularly vis-a-vis workplace incentives" (Gottlieb & Yuchtman-Yaar
1985, 394). The public's behavior throughout the 1980s was but a continuing expression of that emerging macroeconomic attitude.

All of this is not to say that the Israeli public's reaction to its
government's economic policy has become monolithic or even consistently antipaternalistic. As the above quote suggests, "resistance to
government intervention in the economy" is "not entirely crystallized"—even a decade later. For instance, when on the last day of his
tenure as finance minister in early 1990 Shimon Peres transferred
about 100 million shekels to the Histadrut Health Fund in order to
save it from collapse, hardly a public whimper was to be heard. Much
the same held true some months earlier when far larger government

sums were used to save the kibbutz movement from bankruptcy. Thus, the Israeli public has not become an unbridled supporter of Milton Friedman laissez faire in its purest form. Still, when compared with the economic docility displayed by Israelis throughout the fifties and sixties especially, their activity in the 1980s is impressive indeed.

Residual Grassroots Elements

Conversely, the public's clear victory in this general economic revolt should not be taken as an indication that certain residual elements of the economic grassroots reaction will be easily expunged from the Israeli scene. One of the aspects not mentioned above, but significant nonetheless in that it has had sociocultural implications, is the Israelis' increasing penchant for purchasing imported goods instead of their own home-produced products (notwithstanding the fact that many products are not produced in Israel at all). The problem has reached such proportions that the Israeli government in the late 1970s began "Buy Blue and White" campaigns (the Israeli flag colors) to encourage locally made purchases. However, with an economy looking more black and blue than blue and white, the import rush was on.

All joking aside (and it is not a laughing matter for the Israeli authorities with a constant eye on the balance of payments deficit), the underlying cause for this was less the state of the macroeconomy than the increasingly shoddy quality of many Israeli products. Yet there were a number of ironies here.

First, much of the blame for the increasingly problematic state of Israeli industry could be laid at the government's doorstep, and specifically the ongoing policy of high protectionist tariffs to "help" local industry. By forcing the public to pay far more for imported goods than local goods (e.g. a Tadiran refrigerator costs about $1000–$2000, while a GE or Amana fridge of equal size runs about $7000–$8000 as a result of import duties), local industry had far less incentive to maintain high standards (or optimal efficiency). However, once the Israeli public began to reach a fairly high income level with a certain amount of discretionary income in the mid to late seventies, the consumer "revolt" commenced—thereby undercutting the very *raison d'etre* for the government's policy in the first place! The free trade agreements signed by Israel in the late eighties with Europe and the United States (to be fully implemented by the mid nineties), were but another indication that the Israeli government was forced to bow to the inexorable force of the public's contrarian behavior.

A second and even more bizarre irony in this saga was the fact that in many respects Israeli products were among the best in the world! Companies such as Scitex (computer graphics), Elscint (medical imaging technology), Epilady (personal grooming), and even mundane products as citrus fruit and flowers (Israel has sold tulips to Holland and yellow roses to Texas!), are among the world leaders in their respective fields. Why, then, the Israeli aversion to buying blue and white? Here, too, governmental economic policy was at fault.

Because of the great need for foreign currency, official Israeli policy has been geared to encouraging and even subsidizing exports, even to the detriment of local consumption. That this is highly ironic from a Zionist perspective (which prided itself on local self-sufficiency) is almost beside the point. But when the Israeli public cannot literally buy the best Jaffa oranges, Carmel avocados, finished wood products,[1] etc. (because the entire production is headed overseas), then it is hardly surprising that Israelis over time have come to believe in their economy's product inferiority. The public's own response to look overseas, eventually undermined the government's economic goals once again: what the centralized and regulated export market taketh, the public's private import reaction giveth away.... The authorities' paternalistic decision that Israelis were good enough to produce these fine products for export but were not worthy of purchasing and using them at home, engendered a private consumption revolt which will not be easy to reverse in the future.

There are a number of additional areas where economic revolt can be discerned. First, the number of firms (and employees) working on the basis of individual contracts, instead of collective bargaining, is on the increase—especially in the high-tech firms, which the government seeks to encourage as the "future wave" of Israeli industry. Even within the public sector there is a growing tendency to hire on a "personal contract" basis those highly skilled workers it could not otherwise attract. This is a clear reaction against the Histadrut system which places almost all Israeli workers on a parity lockstep with all other workers through global collective bargaining, a clear disincen-

---

[1]A personal experience speaks volumes on this score. Before my own aliyah to Israel, I purchased a top-of-the line teakwood modular bookcase in New York. When it arrived, I was pleasantly surprised to find that each shelf had a "Made in Israel" sticker. After I immigrated and set up my apartment, I realized that my wall could use a few more shelves and so called up the kibbutz manufacturer. Their response: "we're sorry, but we produce only for export." I literally had to wait until my first visit back to New York where I purchased the extra shelving for reimport into Israel!

tive to productive work and concomitant merit pay. Assuming that the number of such jobs will only increase in the future while the lower-skilled ones decrease, the demise of the Histadrut's traditional predominance in this area of Israeli economic life is but a question of time.

Indeed, in the 1980 survey mentioned above, the handwriting could be seen clearly on the wall regarding this most "sacrosanct" of aspects in the Israeli economy: job security. "Only 26 percent expressed support for the present tenure system [for all workers], whereas 64 percent advocated some change so as to make tenure contingent upon a set of criteria, and the remaining 10 percent suggested abandoning it altogether" (Gottlieb & Yuchtman-Yaar 1985, 395).

Second, developments occurring within the bastion of Israeli collectivism—the kibbutz—are an even starker indication of socialism's (economic) philosophical and practical bankruptcy (the movement as a whole has an accumulated debt of about $10 billion, as reported in *Ha'aretz* 10/12/90, 4b). Increasingly, kibbutz members have been opening and maintaining secret external bank accounts; they have been demanding (and getting) greater sums of discretionary income for their own free choice use; and most significant and damaging of all, approximately *50 percent* of kibbutz youth (except for the minority religious kibbutzim) now decide not to return to their kibbutz homes after completing their army service (Blasi 1986, 119)! While there may be certain sociologically related reasons for the last item (insular kibbutz society, etc.), there is little doubt that the general reigning collectivist and nonindividualist kibbutz economic philosophy is the major factor behind this human outflow.

Here, too, it may be added, the kibbutzim have begun to respond in more "free market" fashion: some have begun paying salaries to their members and charging them for food consumed and durable goods purchased; others have begun opening their formerly closed settlements to the outside (e.g. renting out their halls for functions; establishing old age homes); while still others have begun to "fire" members from their unproductive jobs, in some cases even encouraging them to seek daily work outside the kibbutz while still continuing to be part of the kibbutz society (*Ha'aretz* 10/12/90, 4b). In short, while the entire kibbutz sector constitutes a mere 2.5 percent of the Israeli Jewish population, such developments in the very core of Israeli socialism reinforce all the more the general perception of economic grassroots revolt, as well as the surrender of the powers-that-be (on whatever level) to this irresistible socioeconomic public force.

The Ultimate Economic Revolt: Exit

The large scale outflow of kibbutz youth from their socialist homes suggests that a similar, more general, but distinctly Israeli problem—*yeridah* (emigration from the country)—might also be usefully perceived as a final form of economic grassroots revolt. Hirschman (1970) argued that in the absence of loyalty to a social entity, one of two possibilities present themselves: voice or exit. The disgruntled citizen or consumer can, of course, vociferously demonstrate against the government or write a letter to the company's customer complaint department, thereby venting "voice." When that does not work, the next step is to "exit"—vote for an opposition party or buy a competitors' product. But what happens when there is only one company or all the viable parties promote the same misguided policy?

Hirschman's reply (not altogether complete, as shall be explained in chapter 13) is that within the confines of one's economic world, supraexit from the product to a substitute product is the only answer (neither bus nor train serves the purpose? a car is purchased). However, such substitution may not always be possible (cars in Israel cost too much for many; the best grapefruits cannot be found), and in any case when the problem reappears in a host of economic areas the individual involved may not be willing to continue putting up with such an economic system *in toto*.

The ultimate "exit" solution, then is physically removing oneself from the system—in Israeli terms: *yeridah*. The estimated range of the total number of *yordim* runs between 250,000 to 500,000—quite a large number for a country which today still has less than five million souls. The situation in the mid eighties was getting worse, as net migration—immigration minus emigration—was actually negative: an approximate overall loss of 4,750 in both 1985 and 1986 (Rabushka & Hanke 1989, 2).

There is no denying the fact that there exist a host of factors underlying the complex phenomenon of Israeli outmigration, including the burdens of army service, a tense security situation, the allure of America, etc. *Yeridah*, therefore, cannot be considered exclusively a revolt against the Israeli economic system. On the other hand, as the Bank of Israel reported (1986, 82; 86): "the development of *yeridah* is highly influenced by the job market in Israel and overseas.... The sharp contraction in *aliyah* after 1973, and the fast rise of immigrant 'dropouts' from the Soviet Union [i.e. not coming to Israel but rather] immigrating to the West, were influenced by the slowing growth of [Israel's] economy at the time."

Here, then, is the explanation for the fact that among all the issue areas discussed in part II of this book, it is in the economic sphere that the Israeli public's grassroots revolt has succeeded the most, and by all indications will continue to achieve more in the future: the government has already announced its plans for a massive privatization of many of its corporations (Rabushka & Hanke 1989, 48–51); the decartelization of several sectors of the economy, e.g. energy; and further significant tax reductions (especially the corporate income tax, which was lowered in September 1990, from 45 percent to 42 percent). There is really no choice, for the national cost of the authorities not giving in here would be to shut the door in the face of Western immigration while broadening the "ultimate exit" revolt—leading to an even greater future loss of Israel's most precious commodity: the grassroots itself.

6

Communications: The Mess Media Revolt

The Misdevelopment of Israel's Mass Media

If there is one area of life in Israel that has developed in almost surrealistic fashion, it is the realm of mass communications. As a result, the grassroots revolt here was both the most widespread and the most persistent of all the social areas where such a public backlash was felt.

The ruling authorities, taking their lead from the British model of the British Broadcasting Corporation (BBC), established a government monopoly over radio well before the State of Israel came into existence. This approach was continued in the late 1960s with the advent of television—afternoon educational programming appearing for the first time in 1965, and general/adult nightly broadcasts in 1968. (The reason that television did not commence earlier in Israel was that Ben-Gurion simply did not want it. This was paternalism personified. But as Israel Broadcasting back then was run as a department of the prime minister's office, there was nothing anyone could do about it.)

One of the earliest questions facing the Israel Broadcasting Authority (IBA) was whether to immediately commence with color television programming or to purchase black-and-white production equipment. This question was not so much a matter of the small added expense which the IBA would have to pay for color production or even a problem of the added initial capital investment required, but rather involved the potentially far larger drain on Israel's foreign currency as a result of the public's large-scale future purchase of color television sets (which cost three times as much as black and white sets). The political authorities decided to opt for black and white.

Whereupon an immediate problem was encountered: by the late sixties no one in the world was any longer selling new black-and-white television production equipment, as everyone elsewhere was switching to, or starting with, color equipment. Thus, in one of Israel's better kept secrets, the IBA bought color equipment, and proceeded to develop a way to erase the color before it hit the airwaves! For over a decade, then, Israel stood in the unique world position of broadcasting in color and receiving in black and white.

The denouement of this Alice in Wonderland saga occurred in the late seventies when a couple of Israeli engineers discovered by accident what was going on and proceeded to invent an antieraser eraser (i.e. erasing the color erasure). When they announced plans to sell this gadget to the public the government threw in the towel and removed the erasing equipment from its broadcasts in the early eighties. Round one to the public—albeit after taking a colorful beating for over a decade.

This incredible story was but a prelude to ensuing developments. From the start, virtually no one in Israel was satisfied with the general fare offered by Israel television. There were a number of reasons for this. First, the administrative structure which was established combined the worst of all worlds: a large and unwieldy politically appointed board of directors stood at the apex of the IBA, which meant that politics was never far from the screen. On the other hand, the staff was hired on a professional basis (albeit overmanned, due to above political considerations), with the understanding that it was free from extraprofessional (read: political) pressure in its programming decisions. Of course, this was an untenable situation for all concerned—on the one hand, the titular political bosses supposedly ran the show, but could not fire or even dictate programming; the professional broadcasters were technically free to do as they pleased, but had a highly politicized board constantly breathing down their necks.

And the entire system did not even have the usual quality control mechanism of advertisers to provide programming feedback, for the law setting up the IBA (TV) prohibited advertising and instead instituted an annual license fee—mandatory for anyone having purchased a television set. Thus, the financing was guaranteed, and the public remained powerless to even indirectly influence the programming through a ratings system (which did not exist). In any case, the annual license fee was insufficient to fund quality programming on a consistent basis, thereby frustrating the professionals and the public alike.

The public was not at a complete loss for alternatives through the 1970s, but these did not constitute an ideal solution either. Most Israelis, depending on their geographical location, could receive either Jordanian or Egyptian television, and Israeli viewership of these channels was not insignificant. Indeed, a fairly large number of Israelis purchased color television sets in the 1970s precisely because the adjoining (enemy) countries were broadcasting in color.

The opposition Likud, in campaigning for control of the government in 1977, promised to rectify the low-quality situation through the establishment of a second, independent commercial channel. Once again, in seven years of rule it did not carry out this promise—an added sign that it too was not uncomfortable with informational paternalism, despite its persistent criticisms of the IBA as a Labor-infested stronghold of leftist propaganda. It was at this point that the Israeli public decided to take matters into its own hands, aided by the advance of communications technology.

Media Revolt of the Masses

The grassroots electronic media revolt occurred on two different fronts—the one benign, the other quite insidious and potentially socially malignant. With the introduction of video cassette recorders (VCRs) into the world marketplace, Israelis proved to be one of this product's most ardent purchasers. By 1984 Israel ranked second among the world's nations (behind only Saudi Arabia) in per capita VCR ownership! This in a country where the customs duty on VCRs runs into the hundreds of percent (the average VCR back then cost about $1,200 in Israel).

To be sure, this was less a social revolt than a conscious seeking of an alternative entertainment source by the Israeli public. At about the same time, however, another form of television "programming" began to rear its head, and in this case it was clear to all concerned that the public was sending a message to the authorities, indeed pressuring the government in an indirect but no less forceful fashion than if they had taken to the streets.

Israeli law mandated that the government alone had the authority to decide if, where, and to whom alternative modes of broadcast media would be made available. Although cable television had been in existence elsewhere as a viable technology since the fifties, and had begun to take root around the world in the seventies, Israel remained out of the cable television revolution due to the government's unwillingness to relinquish its monopoly over the electronic media. Its willingness to countenance the introduction and spread of VCRs in Israeli society in no way contradicted this predilection for video monopoly, for it was not so much video per se which was feared but rather a competing source of electronic news. The authorities probably believed that the VCR would in fact prove to be an asset in their maintenance of such a monopoly, by providing an additional source of pure entertainment—thereby lessening any pressure for cable television (or extra regular channels) which would open the door to unencumbered news programming. In the event, they were proven wrong on this particular score.

What transpired was the none-too-gradual spread of what came to be called in Israel "pirate cable television" (PCT). Given the relative simplicity of cable television from a technological standpoint, numerous "media enterpreneurs" began creating neighborhood PCTs from scratch. An apartment would be rented, two or three VCRs purchased, and a few dozen (for starters) video cassettes illegally copied. Then the requisite cables (not much different in appearance and size than telephone wires) would literally be strung from the PCT apartment to several score nearby building rooftops (and from there down to their respective apartments)—along the already existing network of outdoor electric and phone wires! Door to door solicitation (leaving no paper trail) was eagerly welcomed by most residents, and in many instances those who refused to avail themselves of the service were either threatened or conversely given free PCT in order to keep their mouths shut.

The result? By the mid eighties, an estimated 250,000 Israeli families were "subscribing" to this patently and brazenly illegal service—about a quarter of the total households in Israel at that time! The newspapers even reported that numerous policemen were found to be subscribers as well. The estimated revenues were in the $50 million range, not too far from the entire annual budget of the IBA itself.

Here lay a profound threat to Israeli society and the rule of law. To begin with, this entire income was obviously untaxed, giving a significant boost to the underground economy (which did not need any more reinforcement as we saw in the previous chapter). Second, it was turning otherwise law-abiding citizens into knowing lawbreakers. True, the transgression was quite mild as far as these things go, but the precedent of so many people openly disobeying the law (with no legal reprisal) could not bode well for the continued (relatively) law-abiding character of Israeli society.

Most dangerous of all, however, was the fact that what passed for Israeli "organized crime" had soon taken over virtually the entire operation. The huge revenues that it could potentially garner over a few years time, were the phenomenon to continue unchecked, would have significantly increased its ability to flourish in other more insidious enterprises which already exhibited preliminary signs of illicit activity (e.g. drugs).

Why were so many Israelis willing to be a part of such an obviously illegal phenomenon? One answer has already been hinted at—the inability of the authorities to do much about the PCTs. Notwithstanding numerous raids and police campaigns to root out the PCTs, the problem proved to be as intractable as pulling out all mushrooms sprouting after every rainfall. Even confiscation of the equipment was of little avail, as a few thousand dollars was sufficient to reset up shop in the same neighborhood within several days. More to the point, the police did not dare to try and punish the subscribers, so what was there to lose if no personal cost was apparent and service was "guaranteed" despite the authorities' best (albeit sporadic) efforts?

Second, the hunger for leisure entertainment was inexhaustible after years of programming barrenness. Except for some specific rare situations, the IBA had a policy of not screening movies less than a decade old! With original Israeli programming very sparse (except for endless number of "talking head" interview shows), and the movie theaters a distinctly negative experience what with bottles rolling down the aisles and the continual rainfall of sunflower seed shells being spit through the air (this finally ceased in the 1980s with the long overdue renovation of many movie houses), the public had little alternative—and therefore few qualms—but to join the PCT bandwagon. To paraphrase an Israeli motto from the national security realm, this was a *milkhemet ain brairah* ("a war of no choice")—in the double sense of the term.

Third, while a part of the public may not have been aware of it, the Israeli media did report on at least one cable television situation in Israel which had received government sanction, and which could only heighten the public's resentment against perceived governmental discrimination and paternalism. Because of the quasi-corporate nature of the kibbutzim, they had found a loophole in the law that allowed them to broadcast closed circuit cable television within the confines of their community. No doubt this was legal (there was obviously no subscriber fee), and even had a certain justification (not unlike a corporation which creates a closed circuit system between its offices), but such legalistic niceties were surely lost on the public at large. If the socialists could do it, why not neighborhood entrepreneurial capitalists?

In short, by the late eighties the authorities were faced with a grassroots revolt of truly monumental proportions, and one that threatened to have consequences far beyond the narrow realm of mass communications. Moreover, the news from the technology front was only getting worse from the authorities' perspective, as satellite dishes also began to enter the fray at about this time. Here was a problem of an even more acute order, for any governmental action would have necessitated going after the common citizen with a dish on the roof—not sleazy gangsters with criminal records. And from the electronic news perspective, the satellite dish with its ability to get channels from Europe and (potentially) the Middle East, meant that the monopolistic horse was already out of the barn. At the rate things were moving, virtually no one would be left to watch the IBA channel by the mid nineties.

As a result of all this, the authorities finally succumbed. But even here it was accomplished not through government fiat, but by that rare procedure in Israel called Knesset-initiated legislation. For once, the representatives of the people became caught up in the grass-roots spirit and moved ahead of, and beyond, what the government seemed willing to do on its own.

For over a decade (actually, since the campaign of 1977, as noted above), the government had been promising the public that legislation would be passed to establish a Second Channel, loosely akin to Britain's commercial independent television stations. Virtually nothing had been done on this score until 1986, when Prof. Amnon Rubinstein of the Shinui party (the remnant of the grassroots DASH which disintegrated after 1977) became the minister of communications. Under his prodding and direction, the Second Channel bill began to make its way through the Knesset, after finally being approved in principle by the government in late 1986. Unfortunately, his party's exit from the government a year later removed this driving force behind the Second Channel; it was not until early 1990 that the draft bill actually passed all three readings in the Knesset to become law.

We shall return in a moment to the Second Channel, for its saga is even more bizarre than already noted, with ramifications which will necessitate an extended discussion regarding Israel's print media as well. Let us first conclude the cable television story.

Because of the snail's pace movement of the Second Channel legislation, and the continued grassroots pressure for greater media choice, Member of Knesset (MK) Meir Shitrit (formerly the youngest mayor in Israel's history, and a grassroots Israeli politician par excellence) stepped into the breach. The result, in his own words:

> I decided to act, and introduced a private-member bill for cable TV in the development towns, something which few representatives would have the courage to oppose given the limited cultural opportunities in those underdeveloped areas.... Well, once it passed its first reading and arrived at the committee, everyone asked, 'Why just development towns?' Before anyone could catch their breath the bill had regional and pay-TV attached, and the

momentum drove it right through the final readings into law. But the credit is not mine: all of this came about through tremendous public pressure (Lehman-Wilzig 1988, 17; personal interview).

The government could not find the political wherewithal to force its usual iron discipline on its Knesset majority. Legal cable television and regional radio arrived on the Israeli scene on Jan. 1, 1990, ushering in the new decade with a radically transformed media situation (a potential of twenty-four cable channels to choose from). The public's interest and needs were finally placed in the forefront, through such devices as public access studio and air time, etc. Nevertheless, these new media merely resolved the public's entertainment problems. While throwing them the bone of independent local news (each cable and radio station receives a municipal or regional franchise, and its mandate is to serve merely the local population without getting unduly involved in extramunicipal issues), it was unclear even after the belated passage of the Second Channel law how it would provide independent national news.

It is the fate of the Second Channel, and the provisions of its statute, which are more indicative of the residual centralistic paternalism to which the authorities still cling. While the initial idea was to set up an independent channel, the final bill enacted by the Knesset did not appreciably alter the political party nature of such a channel's supervisory council: it will comprise fifteen directors appointed by the government (upon the recommendation of the communications minister), with powers which include having the final say regarding which companies receive the franchises—to be allotted by day of the week (*Ma'ariv* 2/9/90a, 1C).

More incredibly, and from a Western/liberal perspective quite outrageously, the Israeli newspaper association along with the IBA argued that such a station would do serious financial harm to Israel's traditional media, and so should be compensated during the first five years for revenues lost as a result of the Second Channel's economic competition! In any case, the newspapers have been allowed to own up to ten percent (they had wanted a ceiling of forty-nine percent) of the Second Channel, so that some semblance of cartelization may still remain.

Press Under Pressure

All this leads to the important question of where Israel's printed press fits into the grassroots media revolt. Have the newspapers been on the public's side or the side of the political establishment? Indeed, why hasn't the press suffered from the same control as the electronic media?

The answer to the latter question returns us to the early *yishuv* period. The Israeli press preceded the State of Israel by about three decades (*Ha'aretz* and *Davar* commenced publishing in the 1920s), and were employed in the *yishuv* as the spearhead against the British Mandate in forging a Jewish consensus and ultimately fomenting rebellion. Thus, with thirty years of precedent and tradition behind them, the private press barons (e.g. Schocken and Moses) and the various political parties which ran their own paper (Mapam, Mapai, Mizrachi, etc.) were not about to let the new Israeli government officially dictate and control their product. *Mamlakhtiut* had its media limits.

Nonetheless, the actual reality was quite different. To begin with, until at least the late sixties, and in most cases until the *mekhdal* of the Yom Kippur War, the Israeli press in general delivered and publicly supported the government line almost across the board. Occasionally they would even change the reported text of a political speech upon request of the speaker, even though the speech was publicly broadcast and part of the Knesset record (Peri 1989, 4). Rereading those newspaper issues today, one is amazed at the lack of explicit criticism on virtually any topic, and this was most true regarding foreign policy and national security. From the average Israeli reader's perspective, then, the papers were *de facto* part and parcel of the whole establishment.

In point of fact, the relationship between Israel's press and the government was even more intimate than the general public realized. For one, the entire military censorship apparatus tended to have a damping effect on "free press speech," even though the military censor almost always stuck to deleting only those items directly related to military secrets and sensitive national security policy (e.g. evolving diplomatic relations).

Second, and perhaps unique in the annals of the world's free press, Ben-Gurion early on created an editors' committee which met with the prime minister about once a month. Here he would divulge "for background only" (in other words, the papers were forbidden to print any of it) the government's greatest secrets. The ostensible purpose of this strange arrangement (which continues to this very day) was to give the editors-in-chief a clearer understanding of what the government's concerns and considerations were in developing its policy. The practical effect, however, was to enable the prime minister to forestall any leaks to the public of sensitive (and occasionally politically embarassing) material, by divulging such material to the heads of the newspapers!

The debacle of the 1973 war shattered any illusions of governmental omniscience among the public as well as the press. Indeed, the latter came to feel partly responsible for that disaster as at least one military reporter had received advance notice of Egyptian attack preparations and had not published them at the specific behest of Prime Minister Meir (who was worried about public morale). Subsequently, the press became more critical of the government and was one of the factors behind the public's declining faith in its leadership.

Still, it would be stretching matters to call Israel's press "adversarial" in the American sense of the term. Aside from *Ha'aretz* (and notwithstanding a few well-publicized instances in some other papers), newspaper-initiated investigative reporting in Israel is not very fully developed. Moreover, what the Israeli press means by critical reporting is usually much less a matter of analyzing the issues involved, and far more a matter of reporting on which politicians have just slandered one another. In any case, the Israeli press is not nearly as critical as it thinks it is, or as it should be (Gary 1984, 49).

Probably most serious of all from the public's perspective is the increasingly obvious fact that Israel's press is ideologically out of step with the majority of its readership. While virtually all the nonreligious newspapers can be categorized as being on the left to moderate left-of-center (which is not to say that they don't carry a few right-wing columnists), the election results show a clear trend of the general public moving to the right through the seventies and eighties. Thus, it comes as no surprise to find in 1990 that fully one-third of the public feels that the media is too leftist, while only 3 percent think the reverse (*Ma'ariv* 2/9/90b, 10).

In addition, viewed from an American perspective, Israel's press today continues to be quite paternalistic in character. Only one newspaper (*Ma'ariv*) has an in-house ombudsman reporting on the paper's own mistakes. The letters to the editor section is given far less space than in its United States counterparts. Op-Ed columns authored by nonjournalists (representing different segments of the public) are few and far between. It is not that Israel's newspapers have an imperious tone (other than *Ha'aretz*, they don't); rather, they take little account of public input and are quite unreflective of the public's general ideological stance on matters of public policy.

Has there been any semblance of grassroots revolt as a result of such an overall situation? The answer here too is affirmative. First, of the eleven public institutions polled in the late eighties on the question of public trust, the media (electronic and print lumped together) ranked in ninth place, ahead of the Histadrut and the political parties (Yuchtman-Yaar 1989, 9). Second, and more specifically, a very recent poll has found that fully 46 percent of the Israeli public feel that "the printed press has too much freedom of expression"—precisely the same proportion who feel that the press has enough freedom for its purposes. This seems to be a function of national security considerations: 61 percent believe that "Israeli newspapers' freedom of the press hurts the country's security" (*Ma'ariv* 2/9/90b, 6–10). Be that as it may, there is obviously quite a lot of antagonism to the national print media in Israel.

Third, and most palpably, Israel has witnessed a veritable explosion of *local* newspapers in the 1980s, with a readership ranging from 59 percent in Tel Aviv to 84 percent in Jerusalem (Caspi 1986, 118). These were of several general varieties, with the two most popular being: regional supplements put out by the national newspapers, some of which eventually evolved into self-standing weekly papers; a sort of penny press local weekly, of which the more successful evolved into papers with significant editorial material and readership (Caspi 1986, 38–50).

This was less a reaction to any ideological bias of the national dailies, and more a function of the Israelis' growing interest in local matters. Indeed, given the sundry grassroots phenomena described in this book, it would have been remarkable if such a local media development had not occurred. In any case, the recent growth and strength of local papers is another strong indication of the public's willingness to create a supplementary grassroots "service system" side by side with the traditional one which is not functioning as it should.

If anything, the public's attitude vis-a-vis the electronic media has been even more scathing. Some antagonism to the mass media exists in almost all democratic societies which have a measure of social friction. Israel, however, might be the only country in the world where the most popular bumper sticker reads: "The Public Versus A Hostile Press" (*Ha'am Neged Tikshoret O'yenet*). Incidents of television cameramen and press photographers being physically and violently attacked by the Israeli public have become almost standard (although not overly frequent) fare. This is grassroots *revolt* in the original meaning of the word!

To sum up, in the sphere of mass communications the Israeli public has displayed its dissatisfaction not only with government media policy, but with the media purveyors themselves. To be sure, the latter cannot be blamed for all the communications ills in Israel, as the political authorities continue to wield much clout—and in certain circumstances and issue areas a large measure of indirect control over the country's newspapers, radio, and television. In any case, the Israeli public has become less and less tolerant of the general central-istic and monistic situation in this area, and in numerous ways the people have caused a significant amount of change through their grassroots activities. It is a story, though, which has not ended, and continued further public onslaughts can be expected in the future.

7

Health: A Hemorrhaging System

Israeli Health Care: Public Ailment

If there is one central area of life where the citizenry living under a socialist-oriented government expect broad service of top quality it is in the realm of public health. For several historical reasons, the system which did in fact develop was a combination of government and Histadrut health services offered in somewhat overlapping fashion. The Histadrut established a countrywide network of clinics and hospitals, incorporating the vast majority of citizens within its health plan who paid for their membership along with their employers (similar to an American health maintenance organization). The ministry of health built hospitals too, in addition to establishing general health guidelines, supervising the accreditation of health professionals, and disbursing the state monies allotted for health.

While a few smaller health plans existed as well in 1948, the Histadrut's Kupat Cholim Clalit (KCC) was at the time the totally dominant actor in the field, covering approximately 90 percent of all Israelis (Steinberg 1989, 64). The breadth and depth of its services were truly impressive, and undoubtedly much of Israel's significant advances on the health front (e.g. sharp drop in infant mortality, etc.) are to its great credit (Ellenczweig 1983, 366). Yet its virtual monopolistic sway proved be its ultimate undoing as we shall see.

The most subtle but potentially damaging flaw in the system was that the Histadrut used the KCC as a tool for attracting members to the trade union. While on the face of it there was nothing illegal or even illegitimate about this, the financial arrangement was singular, to say the least. In the 1950s a mere 40 percent of the members' dues went into the KCC coffers (an additional 40 percent went to trade union and Labor party administration; 20 percent to the workers' pension fund). This meant that the KCC was at a theoretical disadvantage vis-a-vis the smaller plans who were devoting all of their members' dues to health services. Why only "theoretical"? Because until

1977, the Labor party dominated the government, ensuring substantial subsidization of the KCC to bring its per capita revenues up to par with its smaller competitors.

In any case, it was this *de facto* cross-subsidization of the Histadrut by the KCC (plus the the former's strong influence within the Labor governments) which prevented the numerous reform proposals put forward over the years regarding changing the entire system of public health in Israel from being carried out (Steinberg 1989, 68–72). Any such reform would not only have impacted the KCC, but would have also directly undermined the very foundation of the Histadrut's dominance of labor relations in the Israeli economy, as far less members would have joined its ranks to get in on its health care.

Increasing budgetary constraints on the government over time meant that the Histadrut had to allot more funds to the KCC: 60 percent by the late 1960s, and 70 percent in the 1980s (Steinberg 1989, 70). However, not only did this tend to financially gradually weaken the Histadrut itself, but such KCC increases were not enough to maintain its traditional quality standards. This became especially acute after 1977 with the rise of the Likud to power, and the beginning of a reduction in disproportionate subsidies going to the KCC.

By the early eighties, Israel's health system was in an almost permanent state of paralysis, with periodic lengthy strikes by the doctors, nurses, and other health workers on a "rotational" basis. While the ostensible complaints (real enough) were low salary and poor working conditions, the basic problem as noted above was the unwillingness and inability of the KCC to undergo structural and programmatic reform in the way health services were provided. Duplication of services with the government hospitals was but one of the problems, but as any solution entailed reduction of manpower—anathema in the Histadrut altogether—nothing was changed.

As a result of this structural stagnation, the condition of Israel's health care system became critical, if not terminal. According to the Health Ministry's Comptroller's Report in 1987, more than 37,000 patients were waiting for an operation in government hospitals, with the average waiting period between six months and two years (Steinberg 1989, 65)! Nor did the KCC network have a considerably better record. The outrageous paradox in all this was the fact that fully 6 percent of Israel's workforce was employed in the health sector; even more incredibly, Israel's physician/citizen ratio of 2.9 per 1,000 was almost 50 percent higher than the norm for the West's richer industrialized nations!!

From the perspective of the individual patient—even those not waiting for a life-saving operation—perhaps the central flaw of the KCC routine care system was its lack of freedom of choice. As Steinberg's recent study noted: "the system was very patronizing in that the patients could not select their doctors. There also didn't exist a system for making an appointment ahead of time, which led to many hours of time wasted waiting [for treatment]" (1989, 67). It was also highly inefficient and duplicative: a patient referred from the family doctor to the hospital would generally start all over again with a new physician, including a second round of replicated tests.

Finally, and perhaps most demeaning of all, Israeli medicine practitioners by and large do not recognize the patients' right to know what is going on with their treatment, and it is rare to find a doctor asking the patient's advice in order to come to a decision. A recent study found that *95 percent* of the 1,200 Israeli physicians interviewed, opposed their patients being allowed to see their own files (*Jerusalem Post* 1989, 6). Altogether, therefore, it is not surprising to find that Israeli patients are very unsatisfied with the treatment they receive: "a recent [early 1980s] survey indicated that only 32 percent of one sickness fund's insured population assess the quality of care as 'good,' and only 48 percent evaluate the behavior of physicians toward patients as 'humane.' Similar figures for other sickness funds reflect similar discontent" (Ellencweig 1983, 366–367).

Such a state of affairs might have continued for awhile longer were it not for the sociological development noted earlier in the book: by the mid seventies a growing Israeli middle class had reached a level of sophistication which raised their expectations as to the quality of health care, but also rendered them less likely to blindly accept the inefficiencies and stupidities of the system.

(Un)Healthy Palliatives: The Public's Reaction

The grassroots response here was multilevel, with certain reactions completely legal given the system's own limited openings for freedom of action, other solutions ("grey medicine") quasi-legal in the absence of prohibiting legislation, and a third category ("Black Medicine") patently illegal but rather widespread nonetheless due to the increasing desperation of some patients caught in its Kafkaesque labyrinth.

First and foremost, the KCC has been hemorrhaging members throughout the eighties to the smaller health plans which offered patient selection of doctors and other minimal amenities. Reliable estimates put the number of defections at between 10,000 and 15,000 a year, especially in the latter half of the decade. Today the KCC has no more than 80 percent of the country's families—10 percent less than in the early State period (Steinberg 1989, 61). Worse yet from its perspective, as was reported in *The Jerusalem Post*, "the deserters are mainly young, relatively well-educated, affluent and upwardly mobile" (11/27/87a, 5).

Indeed, sensing that a historic turning point was at hand, the second largest HMO (Maccabi) began to lay plans for building and purchasing its own hospital system (heretofore its members would go to either the KCC or government hospitals, depending on local agreements). It has even begun to invade the KCC's previously impregnable territory of the development towns (not the affluent, upwardly mobile by any means). In response to this competitive threat and the growing patient "exit," the KCC system was modified in the late eighties to allow for physician selection by the patients, but indications are that by itself this will not be enough to stem the exodus. As the Hadassah Medical School's director of medical sociology, Prof. Judith Shuval, noted not too long ago: "There seems to be an impressive trend of people moving from the Histadrut health fund to the four smaller funds in the hope of getting better service.... Members may not be leaving Clalit in droves, but the trend is clear" (*Jerusalem Post* 11/27/87b, 5).

The exodus is not merely from one health plan to another. The phenomenon of "Grey Medicine"—otherwise known as private medicine (the fact that it is actually called grey says something about the system's deep-rooted antipathy to health care beyond the grasp of the traditional providers)—entails the increasingly widespread use of nonplan doctors and health services when the regular plans are unable to do the job. This may involve parents occasionally taking their children to a private physician when a chronic condition has not been resolved by the regular health plan's doctor, or on the other end of the spectrum a full-scale operation being performed at a growing number of private hospitals and clinics around the country.

In the years 1982–1986 alone, an 18.1 percent annual increase was registered in private hospitalizations, as compared to a 2.5 percent rise in the KCC and government hospitals considered together (Steinberg 1989, 74). An even greater global indication of the overall trend is that in three years (1984–1987) private medical expenditures increased in Israel from 17 percent to 23 percent of all national health outlays (*Jerusalem Post* 8/24/90a, 9).

More specifically, the Herzliyah Medical Center which was established in the early eighties already performs approximately 5,000 operations a year with the most up-to-date and sophisticated equipment (Steinberg 1989, 74). In March 1990 another such private medical center opened in Ramat Aviv (Tel Aviv's upscale northern suburb), with forty doctors on the premises and plans for the establishment of a genetic consultation clinic as well as three operating theaters (*Ha'aretz* 3/16/90, 4). Most recently—after a lengthy court battle to force the Health Ministry to issue a permit—(*Ha'aretz* 3/9/90e, 4), a forty-eight-bed hospital/center was inaugurated in Haifa, capable of performing 500 open-heart operations and 5,500 other operations annually (*Jerusalem Post* 10/3/90, 9). And all this despite the high cost of such private hospitalizations being borne out-of-pocket almost exclusively by the patients themselves.

However, even the latter consideration is currently undergoing serious revision. Responding to the obvious popular clamor for greater freedom of choice in health care, a number of general insurance companies have begun offering programs which reimburse the costs of all health-related expenses accrued through Israel's burgeoning private health network. To be sure, the general public has not jumped on this en masse for obvious financial reasons; the premiums are extremely high by Israeli standards, as the insured clients have to cover the portion traditionally paid by the employer as well as what is demanded of the employees themselves. It need not be belabored that as long as the Histadrut maintains its virtual hammerlock on Israeli labor relations it will not bargain for the employees' right to have the employer pay into such non-health-plan programs which directly threaten its health-care hegemony.

If such private health insurance is solely the province of the wealthy, this does not mean that the average Israeli with some means is helpless in the face of Israel's ossified health system. It is precisely at this point that we arrive at what has been labeled Black Medicine in Israel. While few Israelis as yet can afford the private insurance payments on a steady monthly basis, many can (and are willing, or at least desperate enough to) when necessary shell out a significant sum on a one-time basis to resolve a personal health emergency. Were this money to go to a private physician performing an operation in a private hospital it would be completely legal, albeit grey by Israeli terminology. When it goes to a public health physician for ulterior motives, though, it crosses the line into blatant (although not easily discernible) illegality.

The central factor behind Black Medicine in Israel is the unconscionably long waiting period for most operations in the KCC-run or government-owned hospitals—up to two years, as noted above. What is a middle class cardiac patient to do when told that s/he needs an immediate bypass operation, but that it can be scheduled in a year and a half at the earliest?

Assuming that s/he does not have the tens of thousands of dollars which a completely private operation may cost (e.g. in the Herzliyah Medical Center), the only feasible alternative is the following: 1) book a private consultation with the head of the department of the KCC/government hospital with which the patient is affiliated; 2) this chief physician, who is in charge of scheduling operations in the department, will then be more easily "convinced" of the supreme urgency of the operation and thus move up its schedule by several months (if not years); 3) this is especially true if the *quid pro quo* entails an extra payment of a few thousand dollars to ensure that this expert will head the operating team. Indeed, in some cases merely the latter consideration is of importance to the patient, for who wants to take a chance on open heart surgery being performed by a relatively inexperienced surgeon?

This type of grassroots circumvention of the established system is not benign, but rather highly socially corrosive. Whereas the pirate cable television station (to use our previous chapter's example) does not in fact take anything away from anyone else in society, in the case of Black Medicine every moved-up quasi-private operation in essence delays the operation of another patient (not to mention reducing the chances of having the best surgeon perform the operation, as s/he is taken by those willing to pay for the honor). Not only is this a classic zero-sum game, but it ensures that those with zero additional personal resources lose every time out. Their "losses" are not small: one poll found that 27 percent of the public living in the center of the country "admitted that they or their close relatives had paid doctors under the table for favors or special treatment" (*Jerusalem Post* 8/24/90a, 9). If the malfunctioning system caused the Israeli public's trust in its health providers to sink, how much more alienated the public becomes with each (literal) passing of the buck under the (operating) table.

Establishment Paralysis

Why have the KCC and the Health Ministry allowed such a pernicious system to continue? While there have been several sporadic and halfhearted attempts by the authorities to combat the phenomenon of Black Medicine, it is paradoxically in their own self-interest not to fight it too strenuously for two reasons. First, given the extremely low salary structure of health care professionals in the official systems (regular clinic and hospital physicians usually do not make more than $1000 a month within their allotted hourly wage structure!), Black Medicine provides a financial safety valve for the system's top professionals. Without the ability to "augment" their income, the most senior doctors would be sorely tempted to leave altogether and take the risk in setting up private shop.

A recent publicly declared estimate by the head of Sheba Hospital, Prof. Mordechai Shani, suggested that in his institution alone the top fifty physicians were earning $200,000 a year (*Jerusalem Post* 10/17/90, 2)! This is an absolutely astronomical sum by Israeli standards, especially compared to the measly average salary earned by their junior colleagues, as just noted. Thus, those running the official health system prefer internal corruption to externally caused collapse.

Second, and from the other side of the fence, the system is desperate to hold on to its relatively wealthier patient-families because the health tax levied is proportional to the income of the insured. Were these middle to upper-middle-class patients to be closed off from occasional favoritism, the chances are great that the current steady flow to private medicine would turn into a hemorrhaging torrent before long—once again threatening the withdrawal of the central pillar of the system's economic base, and ultimate total collapse of the public health establishment.

The result is paradoxical to say the least. In order to continue to survive, Israel's public health system has been forced to countenance the existence of a parallel grassroots system within its midst. Any attempt to frontally attack this morally and socially insidious phenomenon would only expedite the spread of alternative routes to health care (see below)—in a legal direction (wholly private health programs and institutions), but at the price of self-destruction of public health as it has been traditionally practiced in Israel.

The present situation, then, if allowed to continue, is one where the major two futures facing the KCC/Health Ministry are either rapid self-immolation through taking a stand for moral rectitude, or slow and painful death from an unethical cancerous rot eating at the innards of the system. In either case (and the probable outcome is for both to continue their advance), it is clear that here it is the increasingly desperate public which holds the upper hand because of its willingness to spare nothing in its drive for the best possible health care that money can buy.

This is why the latest proposal for radical systemic reform has at least a fighting chance of being implemented, where all other previous ones failed. A State Judicial Commission headed by Supreme

Court Justice Shoshana Netanyahu issued, in August 1990, a massive
714-page report advocating far-reaching reform of the entire health
system: mandatory comprehensive health insurance for all citizens;
removal of hospital ownership and direct medical service provision
from the Health Ministry, which henceforth would concern itself with
supervision, setting standards, and gathering elementary medical
data (which it does not have today); and the transformation of the
current Kupat Cholim health plans and government hospitals into
independent, nonprofit, self-paying (no government subsidization)
health organizations (*Jerusalem Post* 8/24/90a, 9).

That the Histadrut immediately attacked the commission's recommendations came as no surprise (*Jerusalem Post* 8/24/90b, 18).
Nevertheless, three factors have placed the Histadrut on this score
between the anvil and the hammer: the public's shift to other health
plans, the moral rot from within the system itself, and the antagonistic Likud government's unwillingness to continue funneling massive
amounts of above-budget funds to the KCC in chronic (and annually
increasing) deficit.

As explained above, the Histadrut will not go quietly into the
night on this issue for the simple reason that losing the KCC as its primary source for membership and central cash cow would spell the
death of the Histadrut as a major force on the overall Israeli economic
(and not just health) scene. For precisely this reason, the government—along with a significant part of Israel's public—may persist in
this mission. For regenerating the health system would not only
improve one of the country's most deficient service areas, but in the
process (by enervating the Histadrut) it might also go a long way
towards putting the entire national economy on the path to good
health.

8

Education: School Is Out

Against the Stream: Education and the State

Education has traditionally been one of the central values in the Jewish heritage, and certainly no less so for the Zionist movement which had as one of its chief goals the "remaking of the Jew." It should come as no surprise, then, that public dissatisfaction with several negative aspects of the educational system would be met with stiff resistance and alternative measures.

The problems were manifest from the start. During the *yishuv* period, several different school "streams" were established by the political parties in order to further the inculcation of their respective ideological value systems. Prime Minister Ben-Gurion viewed these as highly corrosive of the national unity which the beleaguered new state so desperately needed, and made reform of the educational sphere one of the top priorities in his ongoing *mamlakhtiut* program. By 1951 the problem had become acute for political reasons: the massive immigrant wave from the Arab countries was overwhelmingly Orthodox in orientation, and the religious parties (which ran two separate educational streams) demanded that they be educated within their purview. Such an outcome would have seriously threatened Labor's hegemony in the long term. The government actually fell that year on this issue (Kleinberger 1969, ch.3; Don-Yehiya 1977).

The ultimate compromise solution called for two "state-national" school streams—the secular and the Orthodox—both under the supervision of the Education Ministry. However, a loophole existed for the ultra-Orthodox: "recognized educational institutions" could receive monetary assistance from the ministry, which would exercise minimal supervision and control over their core curriculum. Thus, from the start the system itself enabled grassroots development of alternative schools.

In the event, the Agudah school system grew over the years, as did the financial support the government was forced to give it due to

coalitional pressures. By 1990, the *khinukh atzma'i* "system" (which
included other ultra-Orthodox types of schools, not technically
aligned with Agudah) had incorporated over ten percent of Israel's
entire school population! Altogether, they currently run about 850
kindergartens with 30,000 children, and 250 elementary schools with
an additional 50,000 students (*Ha'aretz* 3/23/90b, 8). Indeed, this
whole structure can no longer be perceived as a minor religious
"alternative" school system, considering that the 10 percent figure
already constitutes more than half as many students as the "state-religious" system has.

And the worst is yet to come, for the *edot ha'mizrakh* SHAS-party
population has been placing increasing pressure on the authorities to
recognize as still another quasi-official system the *edot ha'mizrakh*
schools which are being established in gradual fashion out of the
SHAS social service institution El Ha'maayan. A good part of this
pressure is a result of rather blatant discrimination on the part of the
ashkenazi ultra-Orthodox schools of the Agudah, who refuse to take in
their economically disadvantaged (and thus ostensibly intellectual
inferior) ultra-religious compatriots. The irony is that what enables
them to discriminate with such relative impunity is precisely the minimal government supervision and control involved in their quasi-official educational system (*Ha'aretz* 3/23/90a, 4b). Be that as it may, the
growing political power of SHAS is almost certain to be translated
into yet another religious school stream in the near future.

Grey Education

Interestingly, the Israeli secular mainstream did not get involved
in grassroots activity for most of the first three decades despite the
controversial "integration" policy initiated in 1968 to ensure equality
of education between the advanced *ashkenazim* and the underprivileged *edot ha'mizrakh*. While the public debate was heated at first, there
was little backlash (Halper *et al.* 1989, 271), unlike that found in the
United States at the time: violent antagonism to forced school busing,
establishment of private academies, etc. As noted earlier in the book,
this was not a period in Israeli history notable for grassroots antiestablishment activity—even of the protesting variety. In any case, the ethos
of social justice was still quite strong in Israeli society in the 1960s and
early 1970s, thereby lending a degree of legitimacy to an otherwise not
too popular educational policy.

But if a possible dilution of educational standards could be tolerated by the dominant *ashkenazi* populace in the sixties for sound social

reasons, such tolerance would evaporate in the eighties when the decline in public education emanated from budgetary considerations. As a result of the economic crises in that latter decade, the government was forced to sharply curtail its budgetary outlay to reduce the deficit in its fight against inflation. The two largest ministries by far—and thus the ones sharing the brunt of the cuts—were defense and education. While the former did indeed suffer significant cutbacks, they tended to be in those areas which did not obviously impinge on the public (reduced arms purchases, etc.). Education, on the other hand, impacted the public directly and in the most palpable fashion.

The numbers are quite staggering for such an inelastic budget area as education: a 24.4 percent decline (controlling for inflation) in the Education Ministry's budget from 1978–1984 (Sharkansky 1987, 66–67)! While it is true that some other ministries suffered even larger proportional declines, the effect here was most dramatic due to the fact that close to 80 percent of the education budget was devoted to the salaries of teachers and other educational professionals. As a result, thousands of teachers lost their jobs, entire subject areas ceased to be taught (music, art, physical education, etc., suffered greatly), and worst of all the school day was curtailed sharply to the point where elementary school children were being sent home before noontime! In all, in the years 1980–1986 elementary school hours were cut by a staggering 28.5 percent—200,000 hours altogether (Bar Siman-Tov 1989, 9).

The public's disgruntlement was universal, albeit not everywhere for the same reasons. On the one hand, the *edot ha'mizrakh* were becoming increasingly aware that education was the major stepping-stone to higher socioeconomic status, and any diminution in this area would affect their continuing successful integration into the Israeli mainstream. Secondly, the Israeli elementary school teaching profession is preponderately staffed by them, and such manpower cuts meant that they would suffer disproportionately from the employment standpoint.

On the other side of the ethnic fence, the *ashkenazim* were no less concerned about the cutbacks. Having finally made it into what can only be defined in American terms as the upper middle class (Israeli-style "yuppies"), an expansion of educational opportunities was what they expected for their children—not program reduction. Second, given the increasing number of women entering the workforce (disproportionately *ashkenazi*), the reduction in school hours and noon release of the children made it all but impossible for these mothers to continue working even part time (in many Israeli institutions and stores, the day is broken into two parts: 8 A.M.–1 P.M., and 4 P.M.–7 P.M.).

Unfortunately, despite the congruence of their mutual desire in this regard, the general difference in *ashkenazi* and *edot ha'mizrakh* resources caused a sharp split in the general public's ranks once the outlines of the grassroots reaction became apparent.

The Israeli cadence of weekday life had always been punctuated by afternoon *khugim:* postschool, extracurricular cultural activities of song, dance, arts, crafts, etc. In most cases these would take place in community centers and/or within institutional venues such as the boy/girl scouts, etc. Thus, the natural inclination of Israeli parents was to seek out remedies along these traditional lines.

The seemingly simple answer lay in what ultimately came to be called *kinukh aphor* (grey education): parents banding together to pay for extra afternoon classes for their children (either by extending the school day or later in the afternoon). A comprehensive 1988–89 survey found that *khinukh aphor* had spread to approximately 38 percent of all elementary schools in the public system (Bar Siman-Tov 1989, 7). The problems (and the overall reason that the morally invidious "grey" nomenclature was attached to it), involved ethics, law, public policy, and social philosophy.

Because these afterschool programs were paid for by the participating parents, such an approach in effect meant that not all children could partake of the benefits. This was a direct threat to the "social integration" educational policy pushed by the Education Ministry since the sixties. The fact that the phenomenon was more prevalent in the country's central regions (more heavily populated by *ashkenazim*) and less common in the *edot ha'mizrakh* periphery (Bar Siman-Tov 1989, 7), only heightened the concern from a national perspective.

Worse yet, these classes were more often than not held on school premises, thereby seemingly involving the authorities in a program which undermined their stated socioeducational philosophy. To be sure, there was also a legal problem in this use of school facilities— usually circumvented by certain "payments" to various funds at the school's disposal for miscellaneous expenses (e.g. special maintenance). Unfortunately, these on occasion led to even greater abuses; for instance, school principals taking personal payment for having to stay "extra hours" (*Ha'aretz* 3/9/90, 3)—one of the reasons that many school heads did not try to stop the "illegal" use of the school's premises by the "enrichment" groups.

To the parents with means, most of these considerations were of little concern to them. From their perspective, the government had shortchanged them in one of the most central areas of public life, and anything not patently illegal was fair game. Questions of social policy and the legal niceties of who exactly was in charge of the local school premises were mere inconveniences in the face of the far greater threat of a whole generation being reduced to semiliteracy. Indeed, the Education Ministry's annual budget battle with the Finance Ministry and the former's public complaints that the Israeli government was shortsightedly mortgaging the nation's future by this policy, only lent further moral justification to their cause.

Nevertheless, on the whole the Education Ministry was antagonistic to the "grey education" phenomenon for reasons which went beyond the undermining of social integration. From its perspective, the parents were pressuring the wrong address, for it was the government which constituted the real culprit in its misguided policy of incessant education budget cutbacks. Instead of circumventing the problem in the field, reasoned the Education Ministry, the nation's parents should be storming the legislative barricades and insisting on the restoration of the lost hours and teachers.

Here once again we can see that the public was one stage ahead of the authorities. As noted in chapter 2, whereas the seventies were marked by large scale public protests along a host of issues, the citizenry's inability to cause significant reform through such extraparliamentary pressure led to a change of tactics in the eighties: the establishment of alternative systems. Now it was the Education Ministry (in this specific case, the antiestablishment party to the conflict) calling for protest pressure, while the public—realizing the short-term futility of such pressure—went its own successfully proven way.

The irony was that over the long term it was precisely such circumvention and potential undermining of the established system (i.e. "grey education") which forced the government to backtrack. In light of the massive revolt on the part of parents who would brook no loss of education for their children, and in the face of a potentially serious social cleavage, the money was somehow found in the late eighties (despite the continuing tight budgetary constraints on all other ministries) for the gradual restoration of the regular school day. The 1990–91 budget called for the return of the "long" school day in selected underprivileged areas (development towns, etc.), with the rest of the country due to come on stream by 1993.

Parental Initiative: The 25 Percent Solution

At the same time that Israel's parents were becoming increasingly concerned about the quantitative reduction in their children's education, a growing number had begun worrying about qualitative matters—especially with regard to the ethnic-cultural content of the curriculum. In a sense, this was the obverse side of the ultra-Orthodox desire for even more religious instruction than the state-religious schools could give; here the secular and/or traditional parents were looking for a means to inject greater Jewish content into the state secular schools' curriculum.

Ironically, it was the State Education Law itself which provided the opportunity for this: by law, up to 25 percent of a school's curriculum could be determined by the parents themselves (in consultation with the requisite educational authorities). This was a provision designed to ameliorate the possibility of educational rigidity and overuniformity in light of *mamlakhtiut* consolidation. Diverse populations across the country, each respectively relatively homogeneous, would be able under this clause to tailor a certain portion of their curriculum to fit their ideological or ethnic/cultural requirements. It was designed to be a sop (although undoubtedly educationally legitimate) to those who lost heavily in the "destreaming" of Israel's educational system.

No one could have envisioned that the major use of this provision (beside the kibbutzim utilizing it for socialist inculcation) ultimately would be to introduce religious education into the secular system. In retrospect, though, such an outcome was not altogether surprising given the religious orientation of the Israeli population. As will be discussed at some length in the next chapter, the largest group in Israel is the one defining itself as "traditional" (not strictly observant, but not secular either); a significant proportion of them have children attending the secular school system. Moreover, even on the secular side of the spectrum there was a dawning realization in the eighties that the complete renunciation and ignorance of anything "traditionally Jewish" was proving to be nationally counterproductive. Israeli youth brought up with little or no knowledge had begun leaving the country in disturbing numbers; if Israel was merely a country like all other countries, why stay when the living is easier overseas?

Thus, in the late seventies, was born TALI (*Tigbur Limudei Yahadut:* "enriched Jewish studies"), which by 1990 had been instituted in ten schools and seven kindergartens across the country. In some cases, an entire school was established or transformed along TALI lines; in others, a special "track" was instituted in an existing secular school.

While the number was not proportionally large in and of itself (3,000 students were enrolled by 1990), the TALI phenomenon was still quite impressive given the obstacles presented to those wishing to institute such a program: obtaining the agreement of a majority of the parents; overcoming the antagonism of the secular establishment (which viewed any "religious" indoctrination with a jaundiced eye) as well as the Orthodox establishment (which probably prefers total secularism to any other approach which might compete on its own religious turf); devising curriculum in conjunction with the educational establishment (not altogether pleased about losing curricular autonomy); and getting the teachers to implement it as designed.

Although the TALI program was not strictly "religious" in orientation, it was heavily cultural: teaching the students about Jewish history, the traditional customs, the biblical canon and the development of the commandments, etc. If Zionism constituted a revolt against the religious obscurantism of the Jewish masses back in the late nineteenth century, a good portion of the Zionist public almost 100 years later had begun revolting against Zionism's equally mindless secular know-nothingism.

Less widespread, but potentially no less important, was the establishment of a Conservative (Masorati) movement school in Jerusalem. Once again, this religious aspect will be addressed more fully in the next chapter, but suffice it to say at this point that given the organizational and financial strength of its sister movement in the United States (the largest of all the Jewish denominations), here lies the kernel for yet another religious-education "stream" in the future. For now, it at least further reinforces the movement towards educational pluralism based on religious orientation that is growing in strength through TALI, *khinukh atzma'i*, and SHAS programs and institutions.

Higher Education: Nonuniversal Universities

The budget crunch, which affected primary and secondary education in the eighties, hit Israel's universities as well. However, given several other related factors, the public revolt against problematic conditions in this area did not manifest themselves until much later. For one, the universities—which are all quasi-State institutions receiving about half of their budget from the government—could (and did) absorb a certain reduction in revenues through cutting research, library acquisitions, and other capital-intensive expenditures which did not directly (or at least obviously) impinge on the quantity or quality of higher education. Second, with Israel in a situation of almost perpetual underemployment until the mid eighties, there did not exist serious pressure for gaining entry into the halls of academe in order to pursue a career.

By the end of the latter decade, however, several elements came to a head: the universities drew a "red line" regarding further reductions in government aid, and began to pursue a policy of "no growth" with regard to the student population. On the other hand, the demand for entry into the halls of academe increased greatly in a situation of rising unemployment, as the bachelor's degree became the central entry card into the tight job market. Moreover, the increasing bankruptcies of the more traditional industries (e.g. textiles), coupled with highly publicized statements about the need for high-tech industries in the future, were obvious auguries that the future of the Israeli economy would be in the hands of highly skilled scientists, technocrats, managers, and financiers. Simple street smarts would no longer do as in the pioneering past.

The admission numbers in 1988 tell a sad and (for greater numbers of Israelis) frustrating story: of approximately 3,000 candidates to medical (and related) schools, only 852 gained entry (29 percent of the total); in law, less than 20 percent were accepted; even in the humanities, fully 45 percent were rejected for reasons of lack of space. Altogether, 11,500 Israeli students were unable to enter the university in 1988, despite the fact that very few had really low psychometric test scores and poor high school grades (*Ha'aretz* 3/30/90, 22).

Moreover, the situation is about to become even more critical, given the massive influx of Russian Jews in the early 1990s—a group which is not only highly educated, but expects its progeny to continue along the same path. By all accounts, their children will probably score higher as a group than the native Israelis on the university entrance requirements, thereby putting the authorities in the untenable situation of accepting the immigrants at the expense of the natives.

But where is there a possible solution, given the ongoing exigencies of national budgetary self-control? The answer lies in the peculiar nature of Israeli higher education: there are no regular colleges, only "research universities" in which the teaching load is but half that found in the former type of institution. And the universities, headed by the Council for Higher Education, have been consistently against the formation of such colleges which might threaten their status and inject a modicum of competition into the Israeli higher education system.

The only successful inroad heretofore was the establishment of the Open University in the 1970s, receiving academic accreditation a decade later. This correspondence-style university geared to the older working student (although a very large number of Israel's regular university students are married and work at least part time as well), proved to be so successful that by the late eighties it had approximately eighteen thousand students taking its courses at any one time—a number that surpassed even the student population (admittedly full time) of Israel's largest postsecondary institution, Tel Aviv University.

But this wasn't enough (for one, the Open University grants only a general B.A., considered inferior by Israel's vocationally minded student body). As a result, by the turn of the decade public pressure had begun to build to the point where protest demonstrations broke out for the first time in Israel's history not on the issue of too high tuition, but rather due to the inability of many to be afforded the opportunity to pay any tuition at all. In March 1990, a large scale "student" protest was held in Jerusalem which found a willing ear—MK Amnon Rubinstein. A law professor and head of the Shinui party, he introduced a private member's draft bill which would enable such teaching colleges to be established (at double the tuition, i.e. half the institutional cost per student, compared to the universities).

At this stage it is too early to tell whether such political pressure will suffice to rectify the problem, or whether other grassroots solutions will evolve. The country is already blessed with numerous postsecondary vocational schools, a few of which have even managed to get special accreditation, e.g. the Bezalel college of fine arts, the Shenkar school of fashion, etc. One recent further novelty is a good example of the direction in which Israeli higher education is moving: two adjunct law schools were opened in 1990 by Tel Aviv University and Bar-Ilan University, charging double the normal fee and accepting good students who did not have the top marks necessary to enter one of the "real" law schools. The teachers, curriculum, and even library facilities are basically the same—only the tuition fee is different. Once again, the public has displayed its ability and willingness to pay from its own pocket for critical services desired.

A major factor in favor of all the potential students of the future is the same one mentioned in chapter 5: the authorities are well aware that an increasingly popular private solution which thousands have already taken in the past is national "exit," i.e. *yeridah*. Given America's growing problems in filling their college classrooms (due to the seventies' "baby bust"), ample opportunities for higher education abroad are available to many Israeli students. This human hemorrhage may be too great for Israel to bear (psychologically, economically, and culturally), and it is likely that the national leadership will be forced to expand and reform the country's higher education system in the coming decade.[1]

---

[1]As this book went to press, the Israeli government announced the establishment of a fully accredited law school in Haifa University. In addition, M. K. Rubinstein's "private college" bill was passed into law in May 1991.

Conclusion

For those familiar with Jewish educational attainments throughout history, and around the globe, it seems almost inconceivable that Israel should suffer the problem of "undereducation" from grade school through the universities. Indeed, for the average Israeli such a state of affairs is inconceivable, and more to the point—unacceptable. One could go further and arguably maintain that from the national standpoint the entire underemphasis of education in Israel is extremely shortsighted and ultimately counterproductive, given the fact that human brainpower is the only national (and natural) resource which Israel has in relative abundance.

This is not to say that the learning process in Israel is suffering immeasurably. The Israelis are too thirsty for knowledge to allow a cumbersome and underfunded formal education system to stand in their way. Numerous indirect indicators underscore this: the Army Radio Broadcast University programs are highly popular; Israel leads the world in books published relative to population size; newspaper readership is extremely high (approximately 85 percent of the adult population reads a newspaper daily).

In the final analysis, Israelis continue to learn by hook, crook, or book. Given the fact that we are talking about a nation which has historically come to be known as "the people of the book," it is probably least surprising to find such a wide variety of grassroots activity in this most critical area of public interest and concern.

9

Religion and State: Holy Wars

Status Quotient: A Country Divided

While the Israeli public has a relatively straightforward address in most issue areas against which its frustration and revolt can be addressed—the governing establishment—the matter is not so simple regarding the subject of religion. Here there are at least *two* different governing authorities involved in the matter: the Knesset and the Chief Rabbinate. But it is precisely such a split which renders the revolt all the more likely and widespread.

The problem is a dual one. First, the fact that the Knesset granted authority to the Orthodox establishment to decide on matters of personal status (e.g. marriage, divorce, conversion), in no way removed the legislative possibility of the Knesset either taking back such power in the future, granting and extending that power to other groups (e.g. the Conservative and Reform rabbinate), or on the other hand adding to the number of realms which the Orthodox authorities control. Nor did the Knesset have the sole power to always decide such matters. In certain instances when the Orthodox Rabbinate's decisions clearly violated the secular law in other respects (equality before the law), the State secular court system has seen fit to intervene and nullify the ostensibly valid religious decision. Thus, the very source of governmental authority in religious matters is not completely clear and is certainly not set in stone—a fact of no small consequence, and a great measure of succor, to those dissatisfied with the current situation regarding religious authority and practice (on both sides of the fence).

Second, there exist in Israel many areas of life with religious ramifications which remain the sole purview of the Knesset and the regular government bureaucracy (e.g. it is the Labor Ministry which grants exemptions to companies needing Sabbath workers). Here too there is a constant political struggle between opposing political forces within the government and without, to change such legislation—in both directions. The secular camp seeks amelioration from "religious coercion," while the religious camp demands greater Jewishness (as it interprets the word) of the State of Israel.

The irony in all this constant friction is that technically the situation is one of status quo (Liebman & Don-Yehiya 1984, 31–40). This (in)famous Israeli term has its roots in a letter which Ben-Gurion sent to the ultra-Orthodox party Agudat Yisrael in 1947. He promised therein to preserve the religious statutory and practical situation as it existed at the time, in return for that party's support for the development of the Jewish State (not at all assured previously, given that party's theological antipathy to any form of non-*halakhic* Jewish State being established before the coming of the Messiah).

While the status quo did manage to hold for several years thereafter, the evolution of Israel as a modern industrial state produced new situations which challenged the status quo. For example, the advent of television in 1968 brought with it the question of whether there should be television broadcasts on the Sabbath as well. In the event, it was the Supreme Court which decided the issue in favor of Sabbath television.

But the courts could not adjudicate all the various issues, even given the abdication of responsibility on the part of the Knesset in many instances. As a result of the dual authority system mentioned above, and because many of these issues (and decisions where made) were seen to be of a temporary nature, the Israeli public on both sides of the religious fence found it most useful and relatively easy to take matters into its own hands. In short, the overall system of "religion and state" statutory and political relationships in Israel made grassroots activity all the more easy to contemplate and actually execute, as each side's "revolt" would be politically and morally supported by one of the two governing authorities.

Moreover, the sheer number of people on both sides of the fence regarding this issue ensured that the grassroots revolt here would be quite palpable. Surveys (Arian 1985, 217) consistently show that about 25 percent of the Israeli population define themselves as Orthodox (or ultra), i.e. religiously "observant," while close to 30 percent consider themselves to be secular, with the largest single group, constituting approximately 45 percent of all Israeli Jews, self-defined as "traditional," or somewhat observant.

The combined majority on either side of the center divide are unhappy with at least some aspects of the religion/state situation in Israel. Given the sensitivity of the issues, the heightened feeling surrounding such subjects of "principle," and the lack of governmental or national consensus on these issues, it is not at all surprising that a significant grassroots revolt has evolved over the years.

The Secular Revolt

The political situation on the religion and state issue is somewhat paradoxical. On the one hand, as noted above, Israel has always had more secular Jews than religiously observant ones, and it is clear that the majority of the "traditionalists" in the center are quite far from being Orthodox in their religious practice. Yet for reasons having nothing to do directly with the issue (coalition considerations, the fragmentation of the party system), Orthodox religious parties of varying stripes have almost always been included in Israel's governing coalitions as the swing vote between the two major (secular) camps of each period. Thus, while the secular camp in Israel may have greater respect and consideration for the principles of democracy than the religious camp (religion, after all, cannot be "democratic" in the lifestyle sense of the term), it is the former which seems to have benefitted the most from the peculiar system of Israeli democracy. The secular camp, always represented by a majority of the rulers, has found itself very frustrated by its inability to have matters decided in its favor regarding "religious coercion."

The initial drive to change matters expressed itself first in the political sphere, with the establishment of the Citizens' Rights Movement (RATZ) in the early 1970s, headed by MK Shulamit Aloni. While other parties (e.g. Mapam) were consistently antireligious in their orientation, RATZ was the first to put the issue at the forefront of its platform. Its growing success through the 1980s was an indication of the increasing salience which this issue held for many secular Israelis.

But for the Israeli divorcee or convert who wished to marry a Cohen, for the bastard (*mamzer*) individual who wished to marry any "normal" Jew, for the Jew who wished to marry out of faith, or for the woman whose husband disappeared without a trace (*agunah*) and wished to remarry with anyone, the laborious political process was not of much solace given the unwillingness of the rabbis to find a solution to their acute personal problems. Ways had to be found to circumvent the official religious system. The following solutions are an indication of just how far Israelis have been willing to go in their revolt against religious paternalism.

Private Marriage

Tel Aviv lawyer Yosef Ben-Menashe has arranged dozens of

"private marriage ceremonies" between Jews who are proscribed by religious law from marrying one another. The couple hold the ceremony by themselves with certifiably Jewish witnesses as prescribed by the *halakaha*, then go to the rabbinical court which must accept the marriage despite its proscription (even though the union is "improper," it is *halakhically* binding because the couple had undergone the proper technical procedure). After registering the marriage, the rabbinical court immediately demands of the newlyweds (albeit without any coercive authority) that they get divorced—which they of course refuse to do. The couple then proceeds to the Interior Ministry to be officially registered by the State as man and wife.

It is worth noting in this particular instance that the circumvention of the official system is accomplished by using loopholes which that system itself recognizes. Indeed, for many non-Orthodox Jews it is precisely the Israeli Orthodox Rabbinate's unwillingness to use more of the very abundant amount of such existing *halakhic* loopholes which is so frustrating and exasperating to them. Numerous (more moderate) Orthodox rabbis have publicly suggested ways of getting around several (not all) of the *halakhic* difficulties, to very little avail. Thus, much of the friction is perceived to be a result of a lack of will, and not of religio-legal incapability.

Civil Marriage

MK Aloni, a lawyer as well, has come up with what she calls a "civil marriage covenant" which is a form of legal declaration between two people indicating their wish to live as man and wife, and is legally binding on matters regarding their mutual rights and obligations (e.g. economic). Such a covenant has never been successfully attacked in an Israeli court, nor has the Israeli Bar Association (a bastion of legalistic conservatism) found any professional reason to initiate action against her despite the technical bypass of the law.

In fact, so strong had public pressure become that the recently deceased Tel Aviv Chief Rabbi Haim David Halevy announced in the mid eighties that it would behoove the Orthodox establishment to at least consider whether to sanction civil marriage in Israel! The overwhelmingly negative reaction (by the rabbinate) indicates that this will not happen in the near future, which should only encourage further revolt on the part of the displeased secular public.

Foreign Marriage

On average, approximately 300 Israeli couples a year wed in civil ceremonies in nearby Cyprus. As Israel must recognize marriages which have occurred overseas (much as each modern country accepts almost all forms of contractual obligations its citizens take upon themselves outside that country's territorial jurisdiction), the newlywed couple returns to Israel and is automatically registered as married by the Interior Ministry.

Others have gone even further—literally and figuratively. Paraguay permits "long distance" marriage by proxy, and this too has been chosen as a fast and inexpensive route for those wishing to beat the system without leaving the country (a problem if one of the spouses is not an Israeli citizen, and worries about the willingness of the authorities to allow them to return).

What the Paraguay, Cyprus, and civil marriage routes have in common is the exploitation of the division between the two authorities mentioned at the start of the chapter. Even though it is the rabbinate which must perform the actual marriage ceremony, it is the Interior Ministry (whether run by a religious cabinet minister or not) which must perform its mandated duty on the basis of the secular law granting its authority. By playing one off the other, or by bypassing one authority with a specific act but utilizing the other when little difficulty will be encountered there, the Israelis have been able to undermine the exclusivity of religious authority.

This is especially noticeable on the other side of the nuptial divide—divorce. Here the Israeli system is truly dual-track, for the venue where divorce proceedings are initiated will usually be the venue granting the ultimate divorce (despite the religious requirement that the husband physically hand over a bill of divorce in order for it to be valid and final). Increasingly, women (especially, because they are at a disadvantage in the religious court system) file for divorce in the civil courts where they are sure to receive fairer treatment regarding such matters such as alimony and child custody.

All this is not to suggest that the entire warfront in religious matters involves the question of marital relationships. Along a host of other issue areas one can see the revolt heating up over the last decade and a half.

An important subject from a religious standpoint (and for some, with national import as well due to demographic considerations) is the question of abortion. While Orthodox Judaism does not view abortion in absolutist terms (a la Roman Catholicism), there are still only a few narrowly prescribed situations where it is permissible. However, this did not stop Israelis in the 1970s from getting thousands of abortions annually. As a result, the Orthodox establishment (rabbinate and parties) pressured the Knesset into passing a strict antiabortion law in 1983. It mandated that each abortion be approved by a hospital committee of two doctors and an in-house social welfare worker—and then only for the few permissible types of circumstances set out in the statute.

The result? A massive shift of abortions from government hospitals to private ones which obviously were willing to interpret the law rather loosely. Here was an interesting, but by no means solitary, case of two grassroots revolts meshing one with the other. In any case, the number of overall abortions actually *increased* by 5 percent from 1980 to 1988, with the private hospitals' share rising dramatically from 31 percent to 66 percent between those years (*Ha'aretz* 5/29/90a, 3a)!

Another one of the more serious issues which entailed both religious and moral problems of the highest order was the controversy over autopsies, which the *halakha* proscribes except under certain very limited circumstances (e.g. to catch a murderer). As the Israeli medical profession, however, needed to perform autopsies for research and teaching purposes—as well as transplants in more recent times— the practice became quite widespread despite the strong opposition of the religious parties who saw this as desecration of the body. In 1980 they managed to have the autopsy law changed by the Knesset, giving the power to stop an autopsy to any family member who refused to allow it.

Once again, the secular population (in this case the medical profession) sought a way out of at least their transplant dilemma, and found it through the practice of removing organs from patients before they had actually expired! Once the patient was brain dead, but the heart still beat (through artificial life support), the organs were removed—a sort of predeath autopsy. Here too one finds the secular population finding a hole between the secular law (which considered the person dead with the cessation of brain function) and the *halakha* (traditionally considering heartbeat to be the determining trait).

Even more interesting, and illustrative of the secular backlash in general, is that for the purpose of science and medical education there has been no decrease in the number of corpses available—despite the law, or perhaps because of it! Every proreligious legislation wave seems to bring in its wake an increase in the number of secular Israelis who step forward and sign an affidavit volunteering their own body to science—an act which a family member is not permitted to abrogate after death occurs (*Ha'aretz* 3/9/90d, 35).

Sabbath observance is perhaps the most prickly of all religious issues. The contradictions, inconsistencies, and outright implausibilities which exist would require an entire book to describe adequately—

regarding public transportation, work, leisure, etc. Suffice it to say that the political implications occasionally far exceed the actual "transgressions" themselves. For instance, the Israeli government actually fell in late 1976 because the new F-15s flown into Israel from the United States arrived at Ben-Gurion Airport 15 minutes after the Sabbath had started, with the Cabinet in attendance! The religious parties protested by leaving the coalition, and the government collapsed.

And yet once again, because Israel traditionally has had a six-day work week, the issue of Sabbath permissibility was felt no less strongly by the secular camp than the religious one. And with increasing money and leisure time, the former have been fighting back in a number of ways.

One of the interesting areas of conflict has been "leisure." While the television problem was resolved to the secular population's satisfaction, the question of Sabbath cinema continued to fester. Some cinema owners (not to mention other public venues as zoos, etc.) bypassed the problem through another *halakhic* loophole: the tickets were sold before the Sabbath (that was the central institutional transgression); there was nothing intrinsically impermissible about watching movies or visiting animals on the day of rest.

By the late 1980s, however, others began to take a more frontal approach by simply opening their cinema houses on the Sabbath and challenging the Orthodox to stop them in court. This ploy proved to be extremely successful when a Jerusalem District Court Judge ruled that the municipal bylaw (similar all over the country) was "unconstitutional," as only the Knesset had the authority to prohibit (or delegate prohibitory authority regarding) such commerce. Once again, the public had found an official authority to undermine the other authorities on a religion/state matter.

To sum up, the secular revolt regarding aspects of the religion and state issue were almost all peaceful and to a large extent "legalistic." There are a number of reasons for this: the nonobservant population in Israel constitutes a decided majority (although not all are antireligious), and therefore force is not perceived as being necessary at this stage; unlike their religious counterparts, the secular camp's acceptance of the state's positive law as the supreme arbiter precludes most of them from finding any extrastate justification for "breaking the law" in public fashion, especially if this involves violence. In any case, the dual nature of the country's authority structure regarding religious practice has enabled many so far to find statutory loopholes, court-sanctioned solutions, and other forms of "finesse" routes in order to resolve their personal problems in this area.

The Ultra-Orthodox Revolt

While the religiously observant population in Israel comprises about 25 percent of the Jewish population, approximately half are "mainstream" Zionist Orthodox whose approach to religion and state is both moderate and conciliatory, following in the path of the first *Ashkenazi* Chief Rabbi—Harav Kook. Once Israel's fundamental religious pillars were in place—kosher food served in all public institutions, a religious public school system, and certain Sabbath legislation—there was little pressure on their part to force further religious inroads in public life.

Indeed, this population segment found itself in a rather uncomfortable situation regarding the more vociferous ultra-Orthodox: for theological reasons the Zionist Orthodox could not publicly disassociate themselves from the ultra-Orthodox demands for more religious legislation; but the former did not agree with the intemperate and unduly high-pressure tactics of their erstwhile coreligionists, not to mention their opposition to the essential anti- (or non-)Zionism of the ultra-Orthodox. The Zionist Orthodox mainstream, therefore, found itself by and large in the same position as the majority non-Orthodox "traditionalists"—not part of either side's revolt but not completely unsympathetic to certain of (the reasons behind) the demands of the other more active groups on both sides of the religious spectrum.

For the ultra-Orthodox *haredim* (literally, the awe-struck), the Israeli populace's feelings were of no interest, for the issues at stake were of "Supreme" importance. But it was more than a matter of religious natural law taking precedence over state positive law; in this case (as noted above), the State was in any case not altogether legitimate. As long as Israel was not ruled by the *halakha*, it was no better than any other gentile nation-state to which obeisance was paid when not in conflict with Divine Law. Indeed, the State of Israel was in one sense *less* legitimate in that it gave the impression that a Jewish State could be run without the benefit of Torah law. Thus, for the *haredim* it was both a personally practical as well as a publicly didactic duty to force the Jewish State to adhere to the *halakha* as much as possible.

This is not to say that the ultra-Orthodox onslaught was all-encompassing or even consistent by their own standards. Political as well as economic considerations were more often than not intricately bound up in the decision to revolt or not to revolt on a specific issue. Thus, for instance, while Sabbath desecration is considered to be one of the worst type of public transgressions, no significant push has ever been made by the *haredim* to ban Sabbath soccer games, for the simple reason that such a move would render them highly unpopular with the broad "traditionalist" class which constitutes the supportive silent majority in Israel on most other religion and state issues.

What, then, were the criteria for *haredi* revolt? The most important factor was personal impingement and/or geographical proximity. On the former side, the most direct threat to the continuation of their personal lifestyle was induction into the army. While Ben-Gurion in 1948 had exempted about 400 yeshiva students from fighting in the War of Independence, under the Likud's rule (due to its reliance on the ultra-Orthodox parties for maintaining its governmental hold) that number jumped to almost 20,000 by the late 1980s, as a Knesset investigative committee reported. Repeated attempts to have the Supreme Court overturn this policy were met with failure (the court strongly disapproved of the policy, but found it to be legally within the law). The only area where something could be done related to the exemptions granted to girl soldiers who merely had to declare that they came from religious families and could not serve for reasons of religious conscience. The Israel Army has actually hired a private investigative service to ferret out false affirmations of this sort, but this solution constitutes merely a small dent in one of the few major areas of ultra-Orthodox successful revolt against the hegemony of the State.

Regarding the criterion of territorial proximity, anything which threatened the ultra-Orthodox lifestyle close to their neighborhoods was immediately attacked as being an infringement of their rights (read: breaking the "status quo"). Already in the 1960s the *haredim* spent months raucously but nonviolently protesting against the establishment of the first Jerusalem public swimming pool which would allow mixed bathing. Losing that issue only whetted their appetite for further holy war in the 1970s and 1980s, and indeed may have suggested to them that peaceful action was not enough in the uneven battle between the majority forces of darkness and their own small force of light.

The watershed occurred in the late seventies when a road was built to connect the new Jerusalem suburb of Ramot with the rest of the city—which passed by one of the *haredi* neighborhoods. From their perspective, here was a classic case of status quo abrogation which threatened to disrupt the peaceful Sabbath atmosphere they had nurtured in their neighborhood. In response, a campaign of rock throwing commenced along the Ramot Road, which lasted several *years*, in an unsuccessful attempt to stop the road's use on the day of rest. It should be noted, of course, that throwing rocks is at least as much a Sabbath transgression as driving a car (the endangering of life actually makes it worse), but this did not seem to be a significant consideration for those involved.

Similar massive and occasional violent protest demonstrations occurred throughout the eighties in a number of cities on a number of issues: a year long protest against the opening of a refurbished cinema house in Petach Tikva; huge demonstrations against the construction of a Mormon University on Mount Scopus in Jerusalem; disruptive attacks against archaeologists digging in the old City of David (the problem here was the removal of sacred human remains); vigils as well as court tests to halt the building of a new stadium on the outskirts of Jerusalem, etc. In the event, however, none of these proved to be successful. Obviously, more radical measures were called for.

What that would entail started to become clear by the mid 1980s. Despite continued electoral advances, the ultra-Orthodox parties began to find that the political tie between Labor and the Likud was less of a boon than might have been imagined, with both parties joining together from 1984–1990 to form a "national unity government," instead of relying on the religious parties in order to establish a "small" coalition. Thus, with the secular camp seemingly impregnable on the parliamentary and legislative front, the use of political pressure did not offer much hope for major gains (although a few relatively minor victories were scored: exporting all Israeli grain on the sabbatical year when the land must lie fallow according to Jewish law, and simultaneously importing substitute grain from overseas; closing down numerous flea markets which had opened around the country on the Sabbath; and most significantly, the cessation of all El Al flights on the Sabbath). In order to protect itself from further secular inroads, *haredi* society (more accurately, certain elements of that society) began to take matters into its own hands on the streets of Israel.

The most notorious "campaign" along these lines was the burning and defacing of bus stops (in Jerusalem, Tel Aviv, and other cities), which carried large-sized advertising posters of scantily clad models in bathing suits, etc. Whether this attack was chosen for its symbolic message or because such posters indeed were blatant and brazen visual assaults on the *haredi* idea of public modesty, is not known. Given the economic damage (and obvious difficulty of protecting the thousands of bus shelters across Israel), the offending advertisements were removed.

Other assaults followed in its wake. Several newspaper kiosks in the ultrareligious city of Bnei Brak were attacked and burnt to the ground, because they were purveying pornographic materials and/or merely selling forbidden Zionist newspapers. Similarly, bakeries selling leavened bread during Passover were caught by self-anointed religious vigilante groups, and the foodstuffs destroyed (in addition to some mild violence being perpetrated against the owners as a warning for the future). Most shocking of all, national Zionist cemeteries were defaced (Herzl's tomb among them), and on at least one occasion a body was surreptitiously disinterred from a Jewish cemetery by some *haredim* because the deceased woman in question was thought to be, in fact, not Jewish! (The perpetrators in this case, unlike most of the others, were apprehended, convicted, and jailed.)

In short, the ultra-Orthodox camp (itself rent by all sorts of theological and social divisions) pursued a wide array of tactics in their push for greater religiousity and less sacrilege in Israeli public life. Their record of success has been spotty at best, but given the "principled" nature of the conflict from their perspective, such diverse attacks could not be restrained due to utilitarian considerations. Any diminution in such a revolt would have to come from within, as we are about to see.

Revolts From Within

If each side has used an array of weapons in trying to undermine the authority of their opponents, the question most asked in Israeli society is whether this is ineluctably leading the country to some sort of violent *kulturkampf*, i.e. religious civil war. Notwitstanding periodic dire warnings by the media and academia, the chances of this occurring are slim—and not merely because it hasn't yet happened over the first four decades of the country's existence. Rather, recently there seems to be a growing revolt from within each of the two camps against the extreme positions taken by their ostensible leaders, and it is this "internal revolt" which might well lay the groundwork for a future meeting of the minds, or at least a more stable *modus vivendi* on the religion and state issue.

On the secular side, the expanding TALI educational program reviewed in the previous chapter is an indication of a growing realization on the part of nonobservant Israelis that the previous total divorce from the Jewish heritage was a mistake—even by their own criteria. For one, *yeridah* from Israel is almost nonexistent among those having been imbued with a sense of Jewish (not just Zionist) identity. Learning about the Jewish past in Israel is no different from an American child learning about the Pilgrims and Thanksgiving.

Moreover, the 1980s was witness to a great expansion of the Conservative movement (American origin) in Israel, with close to

fifty synagogues being established by the end of the decade. While
the original membership was distinctly Anglo-Saxon, the recent trend
has been for more and more "traditionalists" as well as former "secularists" to attend services. True, this can be viewed as both a revolt
against the Orthodox establishment as much as it is a reaction against
unmitigated freethinking, but the majority of these new Masorati'im
(as the Conservative movement calls itself in Israel) come from the
formerly nonobservant side of the fence, and so are an additional
growing indication of a revolt against Israeli agnosticism.

On the other hand, certain interesting developments within the
mainstream observant and *haredi* camps also suggest a growing revolt
against traditional Orthodox and ultra-Orthodox business as usual.
The late 1980s, for example, was witness to the startling phenomenon
of religious women vying for, and successfully winning, seats on the
municipal religious councils which have authority over a whole range
of religiously oriented services provided in their municipalities.
Despite the initial antagonism of the Chief Rabbinate, another secular
law was used to undermine the traditional (this time, exclusively
male) basis of doing public religious business.

Perhaps the most visible blow against the *haredi* powers-that-be
came in 1984 with the secession of the ultra-Orthodox *edot ha'mizrakh*
from Agudat Yisrael—a political revolt of historic proportions. But
the significance went far beyond mere politics. For the first time since
1952 a *haredi* party in Israel acquiesced in joining the Cabinet, thereby
accepting collective ministerial responsibility for all government legislation—including those of *non-halakhic* provenance. In essence, this
meant that SHAS had *ipso facto* fully accepted the legitimacy of the
State of Israel, a huge ideological step away from the inherently
adversarial position of traditional *haredi* anti-Zionism (*Ha'aretz*
4/28/89, 2b). Indeed, the top man on the SHAS list, Rabbi Yitzchak
Peretz, took for himself one of the most Zionist portfolios—the Ministry of (Immigrant) Absorption—and promptly declared that SHAS
is a Zionist movement (*Ha'aretz* 4/28/89, 2b)!

In this light, it should not come as a great surprise to find other
forms of public regressions from *haredi* anti-Zionism. To take but one
example, recently a *haredi le'umi* (ultra-Orthodox Zionist) elementary
school was established in Jerusalem, something inconceivable—
indeed, an oxymoron—a mere decade earlier (*Jerusalem Post* 6/8/89,
10). Paradoxically, such an internal revolt against traditional *haredi*
anti-Zionism is fueled in part by another revolt—this time against
Israeli secularism! The growing trend of *khazarah bi'tshuva* (returning
to the fold, being "born again" in Christian parlance) is attracting

many formerly secular youth to ultra-Orthodoxy, but these Jewish "converts" bring with them (and are unwilling to give up) a Zionist attachment to the State. Thus, the antisecular revolt cross-pollinates the reaction against ultra-Orthodox anti-Zionism in the contemporary Israeli context, ironically moving both sides closer to each other.

Conclusion: Spoiled Victories

From the standpoint of the sheer number of different grassroots revolt activities, the area of religion and state surpasses all the others in Israel. It could probably be safely argued that the same holds true for the total number of Israelis involved in this revolt in one form or another over time. However, as we have seen above, the nature of the revolt does not enable the revolters to achieve all their goals, as the conflict entails not only the undermining of *two* different authority structures but also pits several grassroots population groups one against the other. Even within each group it is possible to discern a measure of reaction to the traditionally extreme positions taken by the religious "combatants."

Barring the complete "conversion" of the Israeli populace to *halakhic* Judaism (almost impossible to envision, given the essentially secular nature of Israeli society and Western civilization from which it is mostly nurtured), or on the other hand the complete secularization of all Israelis (equally improbable in light of Jewish history), the prognosis for the future is an almost inevitable continuation of tension on religion and state issues, with added ingenious "solutions" being implemented by the sundry sides. But this in no way means that an increase in the intensity level is inevitable nor even probable.

What seems to be happening is that Israel is in the throes of an evolving "civil religion" (Liebman and Don-Yehiya 1983), whereby many of the traditional values and symbols of Judaism are undergoing some form of transformation, but thereby are drawing the general nonobservant public closer to the cultural roots of their heritage. On the other side, the very existence of the modern Jewish State and the continued (and increasing) integration of the non-Zionist ultra-Orthodox into Israeli life, is drawing them closer to full *social* (if not wholly religious) incorporation into the State. The mere fact that virtually all *haredim* today speak Hebrew in everyday conversation (it was traditionally considered to be appropriate only for sacred purposes such as prayer and study), not to mention the ministerial "concessions" mentioned above, suggest that they too are moving toward the center from a theo-political perspective.

Thus, as each side comes to the realization that there cannot be any complete victory here, and as certain social and demographic trends bring them closer together, the distant future holds the promise of a weakening of this particular revolt in all its variegated manifestations. For the time being, however, the Israeli grassroots— religious and irreligious—are burning with a zeal found only among those battling for the literal and figurative soul of their people and country.

10

Constitution-Making: Founding Sons

Israel's Election System in a Constitutional Vacuum

Israel is only one of six nations in the contemporary world without a written constitution. Aside from Great Britain and New Zealand, it is the only other democracy lacking one. There were several reasons why a decision was made not to write a full constitution in the late forties and early fifties, but a full analysis of the issue would lead us too far astray (Rackman 1955). Suffice it to say that a rather strange coalition of forces fought against it for self-interested and ideological reasons: Mapai and the Religious Front opposed it; Herut and the Progressives/Liberals were in favor. The compromise was to write the constitution in stages—article by article over the years—through Basic Law legislation. After four decades, only nine such Basic Laws had been enacted, with the most critical omission being the lack of constitutionally mandated provisions regarding civil rights.

Given the steady, albeit very slow, progress in constitution-making, there wasn't very much public pressure felt in this sphere. Rather, the focus turned to a different but related area: electoral reform. Here Israel truly stood alone on the world stage as the only country with a national (nonregional) system of *pure* proportional representation. Such a system was first used in Palestine in 1918 by the third "Preparatory Conference" (in advance of the *yishuv*'s first elections), which chose this process in order to give voice to the full pluralistic panoply of ideological, ethnic, and religious-sectarian groups in the Palestinian Jewish community. At the time, it had a certain "unifying" logic to it, but this has become less and less the case over time.

By the fifties it had become obvious that "more is less." The major consequence of such a proportional system of representation was to fracture the polity into many different parties and factions. In all Knesset elections, between nine and seventeen parties won at least a seat, with over thirty parties running for election on occasion (Wolffsohn 1987, 20–21)!

On the face of it, this may seem to be a positive thing from the perspective of grassroots political activity, for it enabled relatively small groups of citizens to express their "unpopular" (but decidedly populistic) viewpoints within the halls of Israel's national legislature. The effect, although salutary from the standpoint of these splinter groups, is devastating in a number of ways for the vast Israeli mainstream.

First, such a system effectively sunders the citizenry from their representatives. The existence of a party list (the voter could take it or leave it—no chance for *panachage:* removing, adding, or changing the order of specific names on the list) means that no member of Knesset represents any geographical constituency. Nor does the public have any control over who appears on that list, as this is a function of internal party processes and considerations. Thus, while a very small party may have some grassroots relationship with its supporters (assuming that it can determine who they are), the MKs within the larger parties are at a loss—nor do they have any electoral incentive— to know what their voters wished to do. Paradoxically, then, the system affords greater grassroots expression of extreme positions than mainstream ones. The latter find it increasingly difficult to politically communicate with the central parties.

Even worse, such a system leads to an outcome of about a dozen or more parties being elected to the Knesset (the situation has gotten worse in the eighties), and tends to force the government to include about four to eight parties within the ruling coalition, a situation which causes severe problems of day-to-day governance. Even were the MKs of any party to understand the exact wishes of their supporters, and even if they had the political incentive or will to act in accordance with those public desires, they would be seriously hamstrung in carrying through anything of consequence, given the fact that deep compromises have to be made with coalition partners. As we shall see shortly, the situation in this regard reached its nadir in the second half of the 1980s under the National Unity government, which was in effect the national paralysis government (aside from resolving the two central crises of returning the troops from Lebanon and saving the disintegrating economy).

Interestingly, from almost the beginning of the State it was the political establishment which actually preceded the public in understanding the gravity of the election system problem. The public obviously found it hard at first to make the connection between bad government policymaking and the "technical" issue of election reform, for throughout the first two decades not one public protest demonstration took place on the issue. On the other hand, due especially to the ungovernability problem the leadership was acutely aware of the need for change and from the 1950s onwards serious attempts were occasionally made to undertake electoral reform. Unfortunately, it was precisely those problematic coalition considerations which also ensured that such reform would not succeed in garnering the necessary Knesset majority. Even Ben-Gurion himself failed in a 58–53 vote in 1958—one of the very few times in his career that a significant policy of his was not carried through by the government which he headed.

By the 1980s it had become patently clear to the public as well that the lack of electoral reform on the national level (see chapter 12 for a discussion of local reform), and to a lesser extent the nonexistence of a fullblown constitution, was a major impediment to the proper functioning of its government generally, and the effectuation of grassroots demands specifically. Such a realization was first expressed in the large-scale electoral strength of the DASH party in 1977, and in the 1980s through public support for such organizations as the Committee of Concerned Citizens which set up local support groups, circulated petitions, and organized demonstrations in favor of writing a constitution and changing the election system.

The internal paralysis of the National Unity government (formed in 1984) seems to be the major straw which galvanized the public into action. Here, however, there was no possibility of circumventing the specific problem on a social or economic plane, for not only was the problem innately political but so was any fundamental and systemic solution.

Constitutional Reform: More than an Academic Exercise

Surprisingly, the impetus came from a sector of Israeli society not noted for its public activism, and certainly not for grassroots activity: academia. Under the aegis of the Tel Aviv University Law Faculty, and in conjunction with some political scientists from Bar-Ilan University and Tel-Aviv University, a committee was established in 1985 to literally write up a new Israeli constitution, including a reformed election system (Susser & Schreiber 1988, 13–16; Susser 1989). After a series of intensive discussions and heated arguments, this group emerged in the summer of 1987 with a finely nuanced document—coincidentally, precisely 200 years after the American Constitution was devised—and with a similar level of reasoned compromise.

The effort was well-publicized in the media (and well-funded), with the full draft reaching the eyes of several hundred thousand Israelis. This marked only the initial stage of a long-term grassroots

effort. The second stage involved discovering just how many Israelis
felt the need for such an effort. A survey initiated by the drafters discovered the fact that with regard to the issue of electoral reform—one
of the key provisions of the draft constitution (the other three being a
bill of rights, changing the Knesset/government relationship, as well
as instituting judicial review)—fully 70 percent of the Israeli population thought that the current system needed changing (Susser &
Schreiber, 1988, 14).

Public support was then mobilized through massive advertisements in the Israeli press explaining the finished product, the ratio-
nale for its various provisions, and the hoped-for consequences in the
event of passage. Simultaneously, a number of large protest demonstrations were organized, with the largest gathering in 1988 drawing
several thousand participants in a driving rainstorm—quite a large
number by Israeli protest standards.

With obvious large scale public backing, the next stage proved
to be somewhat easier than is normally the case in Israeli politics—
grassroots lobbying of the Knesset (the electoral reform provision was
sent to the floor of the Knesset already in May 1987). There was no
doubt from the start that the MKs would meet with these "founding
sons" of Israel's protoconstitution, given the impressive academic status of the individuals involved. But it was less clear at first just how
seriously the entire effort would be taken by the country's elected
leadership. In the event, the response was a serious one indeed.

Both major parties declared in their 1988 election campaign platform that electoral reform would be a high priority item on the
upcoming legislative agenda. Moreover, while there was no overt
mention of total acceptance of the proposed constitution, promises
were made that certain draft Basic Laws would be pushed to
approval—most important, that of civil rights (which had been stuck
in committee, in one form or another, since the early seventies!).

This was a major shift, especially for the Likud leadership.
While Labor had traditionally been in favor of electoral reform (since
Ben-Gurion's time, as was noted above), the Likud had come to view
this with a somewhat jaundiced eye, given the fact that they were
now in the political driver's seat. Why risk losing their predominant
position in an electoral system overhaul? This was especially the conservative position taken by Prime Minister Shamir prior to 1988.

The events of November and December 1988 changed his mind
as well, paving the way for real legislative progress on the electoral
reform front. The coalition bargaining of the post-1988 election period
was chaotic to say the least, with the ultra-Orthodox parties placing

heavy legislative and budgetary demands upon the Likud in return for their support of a Shamir-led government. In the event, the highly fractured nature of the election results made coalition formation an almost insuperable task, and led ultimately to the continuation of the National Unity government which both sides had publicly promised during the election campaign not to retain. One of this government's first acts was to establish an interparty committee for election reform, comprised of Labor and Likud stalwarts (headed by Labor's Gad Yaacovi).

With the Va'ad Ha'tziburi Lema'an Khukah Le'Yisrael (the grassroots pro-constitution organization) continuing the public pressure on the Knesset, a compromise agreement was reached in 1989 between the two original proposals (this after the bill's earlier drafts had already passed its first reading before the 1988 elections). Yaacovi's earlier plan (altered a few times along the way) was for eighty MKs to be elected from sixteen separate districts (five to a district), with the remaining forty elected as before (at-large through proportional vote). The counterprogram of the "constitutionists" was for sixty districts each electing one MK, and the other sixty as in the past—plus the key provision incorporating the basic principle that the final sum of all MKs would be dependent exclusively on the proportional vote (the West German system), thereby not hurting those parties which could not hope to achieve district victories.

The compromise plan hammered out by both sides was for sixty MKs to be elected directly from twenty districts (three to a district), and the other sixty as in the past (nationally/proportionally). An added provision of a minimum vote threshhold of 3.3 percent of the national vote (instead of one percent as in the past), would by itself remove all parties which could not muster four seats. Such an overall system should provide every Israeli citizen with adequate geographic representation and with a direct connection to the MK, while also improving the ability of the government to rule as a result of a smaller number of parties to contend with overall (between seven and nine).

By mid 1989 the new election reform proposal had passed its First Reading in the Knesset, had received approval in the Labor party's Central Committee, and was awaiting scheduling within the Likud's Central Committee (increasingly beset by other internal rifts). The collapse of the National Unity government in March 1990 seemed at first to constitute a setback to quick passage. However, the ensuing political stalemate, and especially the extremely unseemly horse trading—with millions of dollars being bandied about as incentive for defecting from one camp to another (*New York Times* 4/6/90, A4)—reinvigorated the public's demands for electoral reform.

Thus, in April 1990 several army reserve officers began a lengthy hunger strike in front of the Knesset (*Yediot Akhronot* 4/6/90, 2), a number of big city mayors established a public committee with local branches around the country, a reported 200,000 people attended a Tel Aviv rally in support of the reform (*Ha'aretz* 4/8/90, 1; *New York Times* 4/1/90, A3), and half a million Israelis signed petitions to change the election system (*Ha'aretz* 4/29/90b, 1)! Nor was this huge number an aberration: a poll found that now 80 percent of the Israeli public favored a change in the election system, with only 9 percent opposed (*New York Times* 4/1/90, A3). Most significantly, several leading MKs, ministers, and especially the usually nonpartisan president of the State came out publicly and vociferously for such election reform.

As of late 1990 the outcome is still in doubt: any future Labor-dominated government would obviously look most positively on its passage, but reliance on the religious parties for maintaining power might hamstring Labor (or the Likud at present) in pursuit of final passage.

Complicating the matter even further was a new wrinkle introduced by some leading MKs: four different private bills calling for the direct election of the Prime Minister (*Ha'aretz* 4/9/90b, 2a). While the MKs declared their intention to get together and present a unified draft bill (*Ha'aretz* 4/9/90a, 2a), here at least there seems to be greater institutional and public opposition (*Ha'aretz* 4/9/90c, 1b). The reason is twofold: such a system would be unique in the world (directly electing a prime minister in a parliamentary system has never been tried anywhere in the past), and perhaps even more chaotic than the present one; some Israelis are fearful of too strong a hand at the helm, given the Jewish historical memory of suffering at the hands of dictatorial and fascist rulers. Nevertheless, a poll conducted in September 1990 on just this question found that 77 percent of the public was in favor of direct elections of the prime minister (*Jerusalem Post* 9/28/90c, 2). Altogether, then, it is not at all clear whether this proposal can be divorced from parliamentary election reform, and if so whether the very strong grassroots pressure in favor of at least the latter will ultimately be able to carry the day.

Besides the issue of election reform, some progress has been made on other related fronts. The *Basic Law: Civil Rights* (as proposed by Justice Minister Dan Meridor, departing in certain respects from the constitutionalists' proposal) came even closer to passage. However, it succumbed in late 1989 to severe coalition pressure administered by the ultra-Orthodox parties which have always consistently opposed a written constitution not based on the *halakha*.

However, given the phenomenon of increasing antireligious counterpressure as outlined in the previous chapter, such a setback might merely be temporary. Indeed, it is the *Basic Law: Civil Rights* which forms the heart of contemporary opposition to the idea of a complete constitution. This is because within it lies the dilemma of Jewish State vs. Democratic State, as most Orthodox Jews suspect that the constitutionally protected civil rights provisions would negate religious legislation which impacts on the private sphere, e.g. marriage and divorce. Should the *Basic Law: Civil Rights* be enacted, there would be far less antagonism and political opposition to a comprehensive and complete constitution being put into effect.

This is not to say that the academic framers of Israel's constitution did not attempt to take into account religious sensibilities and needs (one of the jurists on the drafting panel was himself an Orthodox Jew). Indeed, in contradistinction to the United States wall of separation between church and State, the draft constitution laid out as its basic religious principle the inviolability of the Jewish character of the State of Israel. Within this principle, it laid down the following provisions: equality of State support for every religion (at last count, *eleven* all told); the legality of religious neighborhoods mandating their own local rules and regulations; mandatory kosher food in the army and other government/quasi-public institutions; free choice between religious or civil marriage ceremonies (with divorce to be executed by the same authority which performed the marriage).

The chances of such a constitutional religious reform actually being enacted are rather slim at this stage, and it is clear that support for such a change is significantly below the 80 percent found for electoral reform. The irony, of course, is that passage of such a *Basic Law: Civil Rights* would actually be to the benefit of those having grassroots religious demands, given the relative autonomy afforded to religious neighborhoods. It may be, however, that the specter of religious ghettoization is not one which many Israelis view in positive fashion. Overall, though, Israel academia's studied constitutional effort— whether the ultimate outcome is complete acceptance, rejection, or partial fulfillment—should serve as a model for the more orderly resolution of a number of Israel's grassroots demands and internal conflicts which we have surveyed in the past several chapters.

Constitutional Change and the Grassroots Revolt

Of all the issue areas covered in this section of the book, the electoral/constitutional movement is obviously the one which took the longest to catch fire among Israel's grassroots. This was to be expected, of course, given the rather abstruse nature of the issue, not to mention the technical complexities of the proposed solutions. As one of the constitution drafters has remarked, "the latent support for constitutional renewal is virtually universal...[although] it remains largely unchanneled and unconsolidated, more a natural resource of public life than a finished, effective product" (Susser and Schreiber 1988, 16).

But if the citizenry's activity regarding constitutional/electoral reform has taken the longest to get going, nevertheless it constitutes the *most* important grassroots issue of all, given the potential ramifications of its successful fruition. In a sense, it is the father and son of them all: the dysfunctioning of the entire Israeli system, and the concomitant grassroots displeasure, are rooted in great measure in the inability of the public to communicate with the country's leadership, and in that leadership's inability to do what it would like to do for the public. Any change in such an unresponsive system would inevitably reduce the need for socially undesirable grassroots activity in the future.

We turn, therefore, in chapter 11 within part III of this book to an analysis of other potential areas of grassroots inflammation (in the event that the powers-that-be continue to be unresponsive). The book will then conclude in the last three chapters with the following: a discussion of other prescriptions which might ameliorate the problematic aspects of the grassroots phenomenon; a more general and theoretical discussion of what Israel's grassroots revolts suggest about the nature of Israeli politics specifically and contemporary democratic politics in general; and which cross-comparative lessons may be gleaned from the historical past, and taught to others in the present and future.

Part III

Conclusions

11

Potential Grassroots Fires

The rather long list of Israeli grassroots revolts throughout the
1980s suggests that further manifestations can be expected to arise in
other spheres of Israeli social life. That the revolts do not occur among
every population segment over every problematic issue at one and
the same time is not altogether unusual, for certain problems evolve
at their own pace while specific segments of the population may
come of sociopolitical age in their own due course.

It would be useful, therefore, to attempt and understand the
areas of potential future grassroots irruption. To be sure, according to
Talmudic legend true prophecy disappeared over two thousand years
ago, but *re'iyyat ha'nolad*—seeing what is already in embryonic form—
is open to us all. The following survey, then, is more in the way of an
analysis of festering contemporary problems than any venture in
futuristic vision. While the selection here is by no means exhaustive
(unfortunately, Israel suffers from no dearth of social ills), it will focus
on those societal sores which have the greatest potential of stirring the
public to action outside the formal system.

Israeli Arabs: The Grassless Society

Without question, the most likely problem area—and potentially the most socially explosive—concerns Israel's Arab population. As
a non-Jewish minority in a Jewish State, Israeli Arabs are in a very
anomalous and sensitive position. Moreover, the fact that their ethno-
religious brethren in the surrounding countries continue to be in a
state of war with Israel (at least formally), renders their situation even
more ticklish. Any governmentally unsanctioned collective activity on
the part of Israel's Arabs is immediately perceived by many Israeli
Jews as threatening national security. In and of itself, the rhetorical
accusation of "Fifth Column" is enough to make Israel's Arabs pro-
ceed with a high level of social and political caution.

Added to this is the fact that there was no possibility of any organized action available to Israel's Arabs until the mid sixties at the earliest, as the military government in force was only abolished in 1966. Moreover, the fractured internal political nature of the Israeli Arab communities (i.e. the clannish *hamulahs*, different religions and sects, etc.) made concerted activity even more difficult (Landau 1969). Finally, the Israeli government's unofficial ("divide and rule") complex of policies keeping its Arab population in check left them little room for organized maneuver (Lustick 1980).

Yet, despite all these obstacles Israel's Arab community did begin to assert itself in the mid seventies, a mere five years after the Black Panther tumult among Israel's downtrodden Jews. In massive and violent Land Day demonstrations in 1976 which left several of their number dead, Israel's Arabs protested against alleged Israeli expropriation of their lands. Not coincidentally, this occurred just a couple of years after the first national Arab organizations were established: the national committee of municipal heads of Arab townships in 1974, and the national student union of Arab collegiates in 1975, among others. In similar fashion to the aftermath of the Black Panther riots, the frequency of Israeli Arab protest demonstrations skyrocketed subsequent to the Land Day disturbances and have stayed at a relatively high level ever since (Lehman-Wilzig 1990b, 56–59).

Such protest events, although evidence of increasing Arab democratic consciousness and political dissatisfaction, do not of themselves constitute a grassroots revolt. They are merely the harbinger of the next stage which entails "self-help," as we have seen in the Israeli Jewish case. The potential for this occurrence grows ever greater, given the Israeli government's continuing policy of funding the Arab localities at a far lower rate than for the Jewish municipalities (Al-Haj & Rosenfeld 1990, 126–128), with the "social gap" growing wider over time (which is by no means to say that the situation of Israel's Arab population hasn't improved over the years; only that in relative terms the disparities are increasingly greater).

One could ask why the political parties representing the Arab community are not better able to represent their constituencies' interests, but as was hinted at in the previous chapter (and will be explained in greater detail in chapter 12), none of Israel's "Jewish" parties do a good job either of servicing and representing their supporters. The Arab community suffers from two further disadvantages: the authorities' divide and rule policy (noted above) which has tended to splinter and even siphon votes away from purely Arab parties, and the fact that such parties are invariably considered outside the realm of Israeli coalition politics and logrolling.

One further factor has been a "self-inflicted" one: on the national political scene, the largest "Arab party" for years has been the Communist party, but despite its name it has shown relatively little interest in socioeconomic matters. Rather, that party has tended to focus on the "big picture": foreign policy, the Palestinian issue, peace negotiations.

After witnessing decades of the Israel Communist party's foreign policy impotence (not to mention that of the others representing them), coupled with growing social problems much closer to home—restrictive zoning and a severe housing shortage, poor educational levels (at least by Israeli standards), lack of communal social facilites, etc.—a new force began to emerge on the Israeli Arab scene in the mid eighties.

The Islamic Movement party has stepped in to fill the breach. In almost exact replication of the approach of its Jewish counterpart SHAS, this relatively new party has spent the last few years working in the Arab villages and neighborhoods establishing community centers, building extra classrooms, setting up remedial and extracurricular educational programs, etc.—relying exclusively on its own financial and manpower resources. It has assiduously tried to inculcate among the local Arab populace the ethos of self-help, and the donations of money, materials, and volunteer manpower have increased from year to year since the movement's inception in 1984, instilling a new sense of local pride and personal self-respect—not only among the religiously inclined, but among an increasing proportion of secularized Arabs as well (Rekhess 1990, 6–7).

And therein lies the potential danger. Until now, the Islamic Movement has been careful to preach a moderate message, attempting to stay away from "international politics" (read: the Palestinian State question), and even beyond the sharper-edged elements of Islamic fundamentalism, which the movement in principle and practice espouses today in its purely spiritual form. Nevertheless, the danger surely exists that the sociocommunal self-help of today might degenerate into politico-national self-definition tomorrow. In other words, given the wholistic approach of Islam not only as a religion in the Western sense of the term (the realm of the spirit exclusively), but as a total lifestyle commitment which affects every aspect of one's daily existence (much the same approach taken by traditional Judaism), it is not clear where the Islamic Movement can (or would even want to) draw the line.

Reinforcing this tendency are the recent events right over the "border" in the Israeli-administered territories. The Palestinian *intifa-*

da is not that much different in concept from other Israeli grassroots revolts as outlined in this book—except that beyond the social, economic, and cultural elements involved, the political demand of sovereignty stands preeminent (whereas today there is no comparable irridentist urge on the Jewish Israeli side, for obvious reasons). In the pursuit of such national self-determination, however, the Palestinians have begun relying more and more on their own devices, and have started to concentrate their energies on building up communal institutions which would wean them off their present dependency on the Israeli economy.

Whatever the specific outcome of the *intifada*, this form of self-reliance could potentially serve as a model for the Israeli Arab community as well. Indeed, the original Land Day riots by Israel's Arabs occurred, not coincidentally, only two months after their Palestinian brethren in the territories demonstrated in advance of a United States debate regarding their situation (Rekhess 1989, 177). Ironically, Israel's policy of erasing the Green Line between the pre-1967 borders and the territories has further opened Israel's Arabs to "external" Palestinian influence. Thus, their previously Israel-focused identity has begun to undergo a certain process of Palestinization (Rekhess 1989, 185).

This last point bears some elaboration, given its significance. Whatever one may think of Israel's Jewish grassroots revolts, their goals have almost always been (with the solitary possible exception of the Nation of Judah settlers) self-establishment of (or pressure on the authorities to establish) alternative (or reformed) social systems within the State of Israel, which continued to retain its fundamental legitimacy in the eyes of the disgruntled "revolters." In the case of Israel's Arabs, however, there always exists the potential of such a social revolt degenerating into the demand for secession from Israel, i.e. the withdrawal of national loyalty from the State as presently constituted.

Let there be no doubt about two things, though. First, at the moment this is a distant and still remote possibility. Second, if it should ever come to pass, it would be largely the fault of the Israeli authorities who aren't heeding the obvious signs in the field and reversing their discriminatory policies vis-a-vis the Israeli Arab population. The Israeli Arab grassroots revolt recently has begun to quietly assert itself in the Arab towns and villages in a way which is more orderly and constructive than even among the Israeli Jews. But such reserved self-help should not mask the potential dangers. Here especially there is an imperative need for the Israeli government to rectify the situation before it becomes far more socially disturbing and possibly even politically revolutionary.

Muted Mutiny?

A second potential future area of significant grassroots revolt is also tied to the Palestinian *intifada*, but it involves the Jewish sector. We had cause to note in chapter 4 the existence of a vocal group of Israeli reserve soldiers who are refusing to serve in the administered territories for reason of conscience regarding the very notion of "subjugating" another people. The number of conscientious objectors, however, has been gradually rising over the past twenty years.

From 1967 until the 1982 War in Lebanon, an average of only one soldier a year was imprisoned by the IDF for refusing to serve in the territories. As noted in chapter 3, in the three years after that incursion, 140 soldiers had been convicted of refusal to serve in South Lebanon, while *anti-intifada* "refuseniks" are even greater in number. But all these are only the officially documented statistics. As one of the Yesh G'vul refuseniks noted awhile back, the reported cases are "only the tip of the iceberg," i.e. those who openly refuse to serve. Many others find "normal excuses" not to "go over the line [border]" (*Jerusalem Post* 9/7/83, 10–11).

In an augury of where things might be headed in the future, a more recent trend has begun to manifest itself: graduating high school seniors (to be inducted within the year) are now circulating and signing resolutions to the Minister of Defense demanding that he not send them to serve in the territories. Interestingly, the first such petition was publicized in October 1987—coincidentally (?) two months *before* the outbreak of the Palestinian uprising. In that instance, fifty such seniors signed the letter, with several hundred other youngsters signing a letter identifying with their stance (*Ha'aretz* 10/23/87, 5b). Thus, the way is being paved for a heightened level of conscientious objection to serving in specific areas in the future, especially if the Palestinian uprising should take a more violent turn—with a combination of political and self-survival considerations entering the equation for a far larger number of soldiers (and officers) highly uneasy with the IDF's role in the territories.

In addition, there exists another problem area here which today can be seen in embryonic form. The IDF has always inculcated the ethic of *tohar ha'neshek* (purity of arms) among its troops, and indeed this may be the source for much of Israel's conscientious objection as many who refuse to serve in the territories are unwilling to shoot women and children. More broadly, however, the IDF today is trying to have its cake and eat it too—carrying out a policy of military force against the uprising, while insisting on its soldiers adhering to its traditional code of military ethics.

The problem lies in the fact that the *intifada* is mostly a civilian uprising, for which the army is not trained and has yet to develop a clear code adaptable to the new conditions of civilian guerilla warfare. As a result, Israeli soldiers on occasion are caught "overstepping" the bounds of the permissible—not in their objective actions, but because such actions are directed at civilians and not uniformed combatants. A number of highly public and controversial trials have ensued with several soldiers found technically guilty of "war crimes" by Israel's enlightened official standards (certainly enlightened in comparison to their enemies' mores).

Grumbling in the ranks of a serious nature is increasingly in evidence given the untenable situation in which Israel's soldiers are finding themselves. While it is hard at this stage to envision mass mutiny in the IDF, it isn't hard to project more subtle forms of insubordination and disobedience becoming the norm, should matters continue to deteriorate further (*Ha'aretz*, 2/9/90, 3b).

This would be doubly troubling for Israeli society. First, the IDF today still ranks as the most respected and trusted public institution in the country, and any undermining of its moral authority would be a severe blow to all other institutions. Second, the armed forces are Israel's only true melting pot crucible where virtually all citizens are socialized together in common norms of behavior. To "learn" in the IDF that disobedience is acceptable (or useful), would redound to the detriment of Israeli society as a whole, for all soldiers eventually leave to take up civilian life and/or serve only one-sixth of their time in the reserves with five-sixths in the "real world" of Israeli life.

In short, the present diplomatic and even military stalemate regarding, and within, the territories, may yet prove to have a large and deleterious effect on "grassroots" activity in one of the few areas of Israeli life heretofore almost untouched by the phenomenon— Israel's sacrosanct Zahal. Should that happen, the grassroots revolt phenomenon could then be said to have really gotten out of hand, with potentially disastrous consequences for Israel as a whole.

Not that a resolution of the conflict through territorial withdrawal or concessions would completely ameliorate this problem. Indeed, here the authorities in Israel are really caught between the rock and the hard place, for on the other side lies the specter of violent disobedience if not outright civil war. The tiny Nation of Judah movement mentioned in chapter 4 would undoubtedly gain support in the wake of any such territorial retreat, and the possibility (not necessarily probability) of many settlers violently opposing a resolution of this sort cannot be discounted (*Ha'aretz* 4/6/90, 3b).

In a wide-ranging survey of Gush Emunim settlers in the early 1980s (Weisburd 1989, 108), it was found that fully three-quarters of the respondents agreed—with more than half "strongly agreeing"—that the biblical commandment *ye'horeg va'al ya'avor* ("you shall die before allowing yourself to transgress") applies to conceding Judea and Samaria. Of course, not all settlers would necessarily *act* on the basis of such a belief (indeed, not all rabbinical authorities agree that the dictum is applicable to this issue). The same survey found that until 1982, only 8 percent of the respondents claimed to have participated in some type of "active" resistance to the government. Nor does agreement with that commandment dictate *violent* force being used in preventing such a territorial withdrawal; the biblical dictum is phrased, and generally understood, in the passive sense (although 42 percent disagreed with this interpretation—Weisburd 1989, 112).

Altogether, though, we have here an indication of the relatively broad support which such a violent revolt would garner among significant segments of the settler community. As two settlers put it, the first talking of the general reaction to withdrawal, the second to Israeli leaders making such a decision:

> Definitely the Amanah [Gush Emunim] settlers would be the ones to fight. I don't think everyone in Beit Choron would fight and maybe everyone in Ofra would and everybody in Elon Moreh would. But in most of the settlements, not everybody would fight. But in all the Amanah settlements, there would be people who would.

> I hope someone will shoot him [Peres]. Someone else will shoot him with a rifle...that is what will happen. I am almost certain. There are in the settlements enough crazies...not many but we have them. There are enough people in Samaria that are ready to kill Peres if he does something like this.... Also Begin if he does this. I do not believe that he will be here a week after he makes that decision (Weisburd 1989, 114–115).

Undoubtedly, the *intifada* and its daily indignities heaped on the settlers trying to live in, and travel through, Judea and Samaria, have further radicalized them in regard to the whole question. Much as the *intifada* may have picked up on the general air of Israeli grassroots revolts in the 1980s, the settlers might well learn from the Palestinians how to escalate the intensity level of such a revolt. The Jewish grassroots dilemma in which Israel finds itself on the entire question—

between the conscience-stricken left and the biblical-territorial right—
will probably grow increasingly acute in the near future, and here at
least there may not be much room for maneuver or an easy way to
extinguish the upcoming blaze.

Grass, Roots, and the Environment

Insofar as purely domestic issues are concerned, a major problem area is looming over the horizon which has deep roots in the
Zionist psyche, but has only recently begun to become a "hot issue"
in Israel—some twenty years behind the rest of the western world.
This is the problem of ecology, and more specifically, environmental
pollution.

From the time that the Keren Kayemet Le'Yisrael (Jewish
National Fund) was established early in the twentieth century,
forestation of the country had become a major component of Zionism,
and in the eyes of many contributors overseas it was the most readily
identifiable element of the entire Zionist enterprise. The attachment of
the early pioneers to the land also needs no elaboration, as herculean
efforts were made to dry the swamps and otherwise green the country. The ideological and emotional basis for modern ecology was certainly there from the start, and indeed to this very day Israelis are
"into nature" (hikes, trails, etc.), well beyond what is found in most
other western societies, with a strong Society for the Preservation of
Nature (Ha'khevrah Le'haganat Ha'tevah) serving as the organizational focus.

Yet, the very rapid industrialization of the Israeli economy over
the past three decades has pushed ecological considerations to the
background in the face of economic necessities. But the environmental costs have mounted inexorably. The Gush Dan central region has
become quite densely populated, not only with people but with
"smokestack industries." Haifa and environs, the earliest and most
heavily industrialized region of all, has even begun to resemble smog-
ridden Los Angeles on occasion. The country's central landfill site is
close to overflowing; air pollution has risen dramatically in the 1980s
everywhere in Israel as a result of a huge increase in automobiles
(having just passed the million mark in a country of just four and a
half million people); the Ramat Hovev chemical waste disposal site in
the Negev is severely neglected; and the famous Yarkon River has
become a veritable swamp—a reversal of early Zionist endeavors.

Given the pioneering attachment to the land and its greening,
why hasn't a grassroots revolt occurred here as well? To be sure, a

number of widely publicized protest campaigns did emerge on occasion (e.g. against the establishment of an electrical power plant near Ashkelon), but these were quite specifically and locally based. The answer lies elsewhere.

First, unlike all the other issue areas noted in part II (except for election reform), pollution is not a problem where an alternative system can be readily set up by the disgruntled public (other than water; the purchase of home filters and consumption of mineral water has indeed skyrocketed). Grassroots efforts, in this sphere at least, must be political in nature, entailing a higher level of social organization.

Second, as with all western societies, the "postmaterialist" concern with ecology can only come after that country passes through its materialist stage. In America and Germany, it is no coincidence that such movements emerged subsequent to the successful attainment of the economic "good life" in the fifties and sixties. First one seeks a greater standard of living, and only then does one think of higher quality of life.

Such material attainments arrived in Israel in the late seventies and eighties; only now has a significant part of the public reached the point where it is ready to move on to the next phase. Thus, in a 1980 poll designed to test precisely this attitudinal question, 71.4 percent of low status respondents were categorized as materialists along with 68.4 percent of those of medium status, but the high status sector had only a minority 42.9 percent still clinging to materialism (Gottlieb & Yuchtman-Yaar 1985, 404). Assuming the continued socioeconomic development of Israel, one can expect a broadening of such "postmaterialism" in the future.

The establishment of a Ministry of Environmental Affairs in 1989 was a step in the right direction, although it may ironically only cause greater dissatisfaction in the near term. This is because it is becoming increasingly obvious that other ministries are not willing to give up their own purview on matters pertaining to the environment (Health, Transportation, Commerce and Industry, etc.), and the ensuing bureaucratic battles have already begun to stimulate national debate and heighten the public's consciousness on the issues involved.

Indeed, such a conflict will most probably be quite longlasting (as it has been in most other Western countries) due to its generational nature. As long as the older materialist-oriented leaders stay in power, economic considerations will continue to get priority; meanwhile, the growing and increasingly educated postmaterialist generation will probably take to pressuring the authorities in stronger fashion as time goes along. Indeed, the first signs of this have already appeared in overindustrialized Haifa, with a recent environmental petition drive garnering 40,000 signatures (*Jerusalem Post* 7/14/89, 5).

Is this an indication that public pressure might spill out onto the street as has been the case in almost all the other problematic areas, or will it remain within the political realm due to its singular nature? While there is little evidence yet of the former, that possibility cannot be discounted for the simple reason that one is talking here about significant threats to the public's health (the asthma rate in industrial Petach Tikva, for example, is far higher than the national norm; unsurprisingly, it has one of the strongest "ecology parties" in the country, coming just seven votes shy of capturing a council seat in the 1989 municipal elections). Industrial sabotage, or at least violent demonstrations, are quite likely should present pollution—and social—trends continue to evolve at their present non-parallel pace.

Addenda: Economic Competition and Social Order

There is, of course, no end to the potential troublesome areas of Israeli social life which might spawn further grassroots activity. A schematic list of some other "highlights" will have to suffice at this stage, once again based on embryonic developments already perceptible today.

Despite the trend towards privatization in several areas, the Israeli authorities still find it hard to permit competition in what are traditionally considered to be government monopolistic services. Thus, by law there is no place for anyone but the Postal Authority offering mail services in Israel. This has not stopped several "courier" services (both international and especially domestic) from setting up shop and doing big business in Israel during the latter half of the eighties. It can be expected that such a trend will continue apace, despite certain improvements which have been made by the Israel Postal Authority.

Somewhat more difficult, although by no means inconceivable, would be a private telephone network being established to compete with Bezek, the Israel government phone company. Here, too, qualitative improvements have been made ever since the phone system was removed from ministerial control, but complaints about several aspects of the system (especially billing) have been rampant, and more modern technologies (wireless, cellular, etc.) could theoretically enable the venturesome to bypass the regular phone system in the pursuit of more advanced services.

On still another economic front, there already exists a formidable and fast-growing grassroots organization comprising 20,000 households to fight the very difficult problem of burdensome mortgage rates (*Ha'aretz* 4/6/90b, 4b). With apartment prices extremely high relative to Israeli salaries (the former average close to $100,000, while the latter averages a mere $1200. a month!), and with all mortgage payments linked to still high inflation rates (around 20 percent per annum), the situation is fast becoming critical for a large part of the populace. The organizers are preparing for the day when 100,000 families will be signed up, whereupon a national rent strike is scheduled—Israel's first ever major economic "boycott."

An area of grassroots Israeli activity which has already developed well beyond the embryonic stage is private security. In one sense, this is quite surprising given that Israel has one of the lowest per capita crime rates in the industrialized world, especially with regard to bodily violence and homicide (Israel averages a mere forty to fifty murders a year). Yet the reality (and even more so, the media-based perception) is one of steady increase over the past two decades. Worse, the Israeli police are viewed as being an especially weak public service link, what with a low salary structure unable to attract an educated force, and scandals and reports of impropriety depressing in their frequency and consistency.

By the late 1980s, it was estimated that Israel's private security forces outnumbered the Israeli police by a factor of three to one (Ben-Yehuda 1989, 157)! What are they all doing? Escort service, bodyguard, private investigation, nightwatch guard, debt collection, even quasi-police work for specific communities and neighborhoods. Nor is the problem merely tied to official police dysfunctioning; with the Israeli court system completely overloaded (it can take up to five years until a case is heard), several types of alternative quasi-judicial solutions have sprung up—"intermediaries" and "compromise experts" the more benign among them.

One can well imagine what will happen if and when crime in Israel becomes a really serious problem (by international standards). Of the government's three branches, the judiciary is paradoxically far and away the most respected and also the least funded. Should the latter element erode the former (as it must if matters continue along their present low-priority funding course), it is most probable that an entire grassroots array of private "justice" will evolve in the not-too-distant future. An even more troubling element in the criminological sphere is the fact that guns and rifles are easily obtainable in Israel (given the system of military reserve duty). All in all, considering the flaws and deficiencies in the overall system, it is remarkable how relatively benign the current grassroots response has been overall. But there is little guarantee that such a situation will continue indefinitely.

We thus end in much the same area where we began this chapter, at least regarding the Jewish sector—with the most fundamental government service of all: security. The situational gap between the Jewish settlers in the territories and that of their brethren within Israel proper is still quite large, as may be also said regarding their respective responses. But the vigilantism on the other side of the Green Line may yet be a harbinger of things to come for the bulk of Israeli society. The imperative need for government action and reform here is so patent as to need little further elaboration. For if the State cannot guarantee the most basic of all rights to its citizens, what is there morally and practically to stop the latter from taking things into their own hands—in security matters or any other?

12

Conflagration? Fireproofing the System

The Danger of Revolt: Mitigating Factors

The grassroots revolts in Israel have spread to virtually every sphere of daily life—private and public. In addition, as noted in the last chapter, it may yet reach other specific areas heretofore untouched by the public's dissatisfaction if present trends are left unchecked.

Moreover, the most recent demographic developments in Israel will most probably add to the number of those antipathetic to the traditional Israeli system. The current mass immigration from the Soviet Union, adding very significant numbers of people who are escaping the socialist bear hug, can in its own way only but reinforce the already substantial Israeli antagonism to paternalism and centralism.

In contradistinction to the earlier "refuseniks" who came to Israel in the 1970s, the nineties' Russian *olim* are almost all from the urban middle class. A significant number already have experience in "entrepeneurship" Soviet-style, having set up cooperatives and run them successfully in the years before their emigration (*Ha'aretz* 3/9/90c, 7b). No less germane, the vast majority of the remaining Russian Jews who constitute the future potential emigrant wave to Israel are extremely highly educated, with an estimated 20 percent (500,000) having a master's degree, and another 25,000 with a Ph.D. (*Ha'aretz* 3/9/90b, 7b). Even from the financial standpoint, this is not altogether an impoverished population: about 15 percent have private capital of over 50,000 rubles. All in all, not a group in need of paternalistic control or socialist welfare.

Thus, the question before us is becoming ever more pressing: what can be done to stem the tide of the growing Israeli social grassroots conflagration as outlined in part II of this book? Such a question, of course, assumes that the various manifestations of the overall revolt are potentially (if not inherently) dangerous and socially destabilizing. Mention has been made already of the fact that from a civic standpoint they teach the wrong lessons, and may encourage (at least psychologically) illegal behavior even in those areas where the system works in relatively adequate fashion.

However, to argue that such revolts represent a problem intrinsic to the population is not only going too far, but is an injustice to the Israeli grassroots participants. The reverse is closer to the truth, for the very willingness of Israelis to take matters into their own hands suggests a type of initiative which might be very socially productive—in the event that it could be channeled through a more orderly system.

Before embarking on a prescriptive analysis of what such a reformed system might entail, it is important to note one further aspect of the Israeli situation which tends to mitigate the most seriously damaging effects of uncontrolled grassroots activity. And that is the overlapping nature of Jewish ethnicity and Israeli nationalism in the Holy Land. As Susser and Don-Yehiya have pointed out (1989, 13–16), Israel (and perhaps Japan) stand alone in the democratic world in that *nation* (ethnic identity) and *state* (political identity) are virtually synonymous for them. In other words, whereas most other countries have no singular ethnic character which defines them politically as well (e.g. Frenchmen, Germans, Swiss, etc., are defined solely by their allegiance to the State, and not to any specific ethnic/racial/religious grouping coterminous with their polity), the modern Israeli polity by contrast has no meaning beyond the national identity of the Jewish people which in fact preceded it.

What does this have to do with the deleterious effects of rampant and uncontrolled grassroots activity? Such public action, of course, tends to undermine the social glue which holds any country together. When the people's primary allegiance is to the State (indeed, when they define themselves exclusively through membership in that State), and that political authority is weakened through active grassroots undermining, then the very foundation of the social contract is destroyed, with great danger to the very fabric of society. On the other hand, when (as is the case with Israel) the social contract, i.e. the social complex of relationships, is organized and ordered not only by the authority of the State apparatus but equally by the common feeling of national/ethnic identity, then the weakening of the former need not necessarily lead to the collapse of "law and order," for the citizens at large still harbor a measure of self-control due to their innate mutual empathy borne of ethnic solidarity.

This is not to say that Israelis have no civic feelings for the State qua system. It does suggest that a significant section of the population has an oblique attachment to the polity: "the religious, Sephardim, the

less educated...view the state as an extension of the Jewish community (*kehilla*)" (Liebman 1988, 107).

Here we find the source for the idiosyncratic Israeli approach to
state/society relations—the Jewish political experience over close to
two millenia in the Diaspora. To be sure, the various Jewish *kehillot*
did have a semblance of local autonomy, but the true political locus of
power and authority, of course, almost invariably lay within the surrounding gentile world. While the Jew was commanded by his own
halakhic legal system to obey that governing authority (except when
there was a direct conflict with Torah edicts), from a practical and
communally normative standpoint an ethic of "getting away with
what you can" ruled the day in the Jews' ongoing political relationship with the not overly friendly gentile world.

On the other hand, precisely because of this general external
anti-Semitism (whether in the Christian or the Moslem world) the
Jews had to make the extra effort to maintain internal *social* solidarity
to the greatest extent possible. Thus, over time a "natural" bifurcation
occurred in the Jewish political culture between acceptance of governmental authority (weak) and maintenance of social unity (strong).

The Jewish heritage has a traditional epigram for this seemingly
sophisticated social scientific analysis: *koll yisrael arevim zeh la'zeh*—all
members of Israel are mutually bound up one with another. The term
Israel in this context is not a political one, but rather a national (and
social) one. It is the ethno-national element, in point of fact, which is
the stronger allegiance for the Jewish/Israeli people.

This explains the point made earlier in the book regarding the
Jewish penchant for decentralized governance; there is little danger
that the overall national unity would be dissipated, because it is not
the particular political construct which holds the Jews together in the
first place (Ben-Gurion's *mamlakhtiut* notwithstanding). The obverse
side of this is that there is bound to be less civic self-restraint in circumventing (or even undermining) the norms of the official political
system—both because it is viewed as secondary to the religio-ethnic
"social system," and because the latter is a comfortable guarantor that
a weakened polity will not necessarily lead to unmitigated social
chaos.

In his recent trenchant analysis of "political deviance" around
the world, Ben-Yehuda makes the following point: "actors may consider themselves members of more than one symbolic-moral universe.... A rational and real outcome of this fact is that these centers
and their enveloping moral universes keep negotiating both power
and morality.... This view fits very well into the conceptualization of

deviance (and reactions to it) as a relative phenomenon within the context of change and stability" (1990, 58–59). As becomes apparent throughout this book, the Israeli public's grassroots behavior is to be viewed not as a destructive revolt against the norms of the country, but as a cry for change and reform of the system. While alienation has occurred, it is a distancing from one "moral universe"—the political—and a withdrawal into another, more social, universe of activity.

Therefore, the type of public behavior which may not only be perceived as, but actually in fact may be, a surefire recipe for national self-destruction in other countries, is not necessarily so in the singular Israeli situation. This is not to say that no matter what the grassroots may do, Israeli society will continue to function; it *is* to argue that there exists a much larger degree of antinormative leeway in the Israeli milieu before serious sociopolitical deterioration sets in.

Fire Prevention: Election, Party, and Municipal Reform

Israel seems not only to have fallen far short of such a disintegrative brink, but lately has exhibited clear signs of actual improvement through the development of more workable alternative systems of public activity. As this book makes clear, in several key areas of life—economy, communications, education—the public has shown the way to more efficient ways of doing things, and the government has begun to actively pursue significant reform. Those changes will not be recapitulated here; the following pages, rather, will be devoted to a discussion of other prescriptive reforms which could ameliorate the necessity for further grassroots revolts in the future.

From a formalistic/organizational standpoint, the beginnings of a more orderly system are already in view. As noted in the introduction to the book, Yishai's discovery (1987) that Israel has recently spawned a whole network of new interest groups suggests that the public is groping to find (or develop by itself) the institutional means for the more regularized expression of its political will and/or the social effectuation of things which need to be done (but aren't being carried out by the authorities). But the rise of interest groups will either be good news or even worse news. Good news if the system is changed to take into account their more orderly style of activity; worse news if they are forced to turn their not inconsiderable energies and talents to bypassing and undermining the system as traditionally constituted.

Seen in this light, the grassroots movement for electoral reform and constitution writing becomes critical for "fireproofing" the country against an even greater spread of the social revolt. It is mainly by enabling the public to better express itself politically, and through the people's being guaranteed a far better "hearing" by the elected representatives, that future negative manifestations of the phenomenon can be avoided.

What will electoral reform accomplish? It was already noted in chapter 10 that as presently constituted the system encourages a sharp divorce between leaders and led in Israel; but it also discourages the best potential leaders from even entering the fray. Very few talented people with successful professional careers, and/or even fewer intelligently independent young adults at the point of deciding on their future path, have seen much sense in embarking upon a personal quest for inclusion among the democratic leadership in Israel.

Why? Due to the nature of the party nomination and election process, heretofore a potential candidate for the Knesset (except for the rare major personality such as a former IDF chief of staff or famous general) has had to spend many years working within the party in order to become popular among the Central Committee members (numbering between one and three thousand)—and only then had any chance of being nominated to represent the party on its Knesset list (Arian 1968, 175). This had several consequences: too much time was spent on intraparty matters and less on the party's voters; few highly educated people were willing to take the long plunge into party politics, not being able to be their "own man"; and after being elected to the Knesset, the MK had little reason to service the public as s/he didn't represent any specific constituency, and voters had no way of directly electorally punishing or rewarding the MK.

Such a virtual divorce between the country's legislators (not to mention their general, albeit certainly not universal, low quality), meant that little of the public's grassroots discontent was felt by the government until much too late. Whereas in the United States a local interest group might form in order to put pressure on a Congressperson, there isn't much sense of doing that in the Israeli context given the unavailability of an MK—not to mention the problem of the MK having to hew to the party line even were s/he willing to try and respond to the grassroots request.

This is the major reason why Israel's grassroots reaction to a failing system has not taken on the organizational characteristics of the American and West European model. To be sure, as mentioned above, there has been a significant increase in the number of Israeli interest groups of late. This certainly bodes well for the future, assuming that the overall system is reformed to the point where such groups can take advantage of the new political communication channels which would then open up. But without such reform, the emergence of interest groups will only mean a circumvention of the system even more efficient than what took place in the 1980s.

The question remains, however, whether election reform (and even passage of a complete constitution) would be sufficient political medicine to stem the tide of the grassroots revolts as presently manifested. The answer is no. The new election system will undoubtedly enable the construction of the first real political communication bridges between the governors and the governed. But it is highly unlikely that having three MKs for each district will guarantee a free flow of communication and/or the expression/execution of the popular will. At least two further reforms would go a long way toward ensuring that.

First, the parties would do well to institute a primary election system in Israel. At present (and even under the proposed new election system), it is still the party bureaucracy which holds the key to who will be nominated for its list, although the *apparatchiks* obviously have to take local wishes into account. The advantage of a primary system is not only that the Israeli people themselves determine the candidates, but that they have the feeling that extraparliamentary and/or extralegal redress may not be necessary precisely because of such political power. In other words, not only will the candidates be more closely attuned to what the grassroots wants, but the public will perceive less of a need to undermine a system which it in part controls.

Is this merely an academic fantasy? Not at all. After several years of deep soul-searching—not to mention having to survive as a second-class governing party, and most recently in the opposition wilderness—the Labor party in late 1990 voted to institute primary elections for *all* its officials: those who wish to run for the Knesset, Histadrut, Worker's Council, and a host of others (*Ha'aretz* 10/19/90, 5a). This is a major breakthrough, and can even be seen as the victory of the party's grassroots rank and file who have been shut out of the important decisionmaking processes for decades. It is quite likely that the Likud will follow suit, especially if it wishes to retain its image of being Israel's leading "populist" party.

A complementary second reform occasionally bandied about in Israel would be institutionalization of the referendum, or public initiative. Without getting bogged down in the details of such a procedure (there are numerous possibilities regarding how this can work), affording the public the opportunity in certain circumstances of passing legislation or binding resolutions in order to change the system (whether economic, social, or political), would negate much of its present need to do the kinds of things described in this book. To take but one example, there is little doubt that the public would have over-whelmingly forced the authorities to establish a Second Channel and cable television network well before the time that legislative process in fact did begin to unfold, and possibly even before the pirate cable television "network" began to emerge.

Undoubtedly, a referendum system is somewhat of a "radical" suggestion in the Israeli context as it would publicly mark the official nail in the country's paternalistic coffin. But why not systematize a situation which *de facto* exists in any case today in very disorderly fashion?

Would the public be in favor of all of these changes? This is obvi-ously a rhetorical question, and not just because of the massive elec-toral reform protests in early 1990, or the fact that Israelis are working in socioeconomically grassroots fashion in any case. The fact of the matter is that significant electoral and political-systemic reform has already occurred in Israel on a different level, with impressive results. This experience not only suggests that the above recommendations would be met with great approval, but in and of itself constitutes a final prescription which needs only to be continued and expanded.

The reference is to reform on the local government level. As a result of the abysmal functioning of the municipal councils and their selected mayors in Israel during the first three decades of the coun-try's existence, a different system was instituted in 1978 which enabled the public to directly elect its local mayor in place of the pre-vious system which paralleled the national system of proportional representation and indirect chief executive selection. The results were not slow in coming: the number of local councils being disbanded by the Interior Minister due to their maladministration and malfeasance (an almost annual occurrence before 1978) has plummetted in the Jewish sector through the 1980s. But improved local government administration was but half the story.

It is on the local level that we find the only form of political experimentation in Israel, as several types of voluntary committees and councils have been established over the years to attract public par-ticipation in the local decisionmaking arena (Elazar 1988). As a result, the frequency of protest events directed against the local authorities plummeted in comparison with those against the central authorities where no reform was instituted (Lehman-Wilzig 1990b, 100).

In great part this was due to (and further reinforced by) Israel's Diaspora-funded Project Renewal,which commenced in the late 1970s and continues to run over a decade later. Most public attention has generally focussed on Project Renewal's urban rehabilitation of the neighborhoods' physical environment. However, no less significant has been its sociopolitical program educating the underprivileged residents in communal political organization, in conjunction with their respective municipal authorities (King *et al* 1987, 81–96). This is true grassroots development in the political sense of the term, and it has enabled these citizens to get things done through the formal political channels of their local government without having to resort to protests and/or other forms of illegal "self-help." Not coincidentally, social-issue protest in the period 1979-1986 dropped to only 28.1 percent of all protest issues, as compared to 37.7 percent from 1949–1978 (Lehman-Wilzig 1990b, 30–41).

Overall, then, devolution of power and authority to Israel's municipalities would go a long way towards making the system more responsive to the public's needs and wishes, thereby obviating the citizens' felt necessity to take matters into their own hands. Put another way, Israel cannot hope to expunge the grassroots urge—and should not. Rather, what is called for is the transferral of such grassroots activity from the socioeconomic arena to the more formalized and institutionalized political realm. Electoral reform, party reform, and especially decentralization reform, are all means to that end—means that have already largely begun to prove themselves in the recent past.

Planning for the Future

There remains one last element of systemic reform in Israel which cuts across all levels of government and their sundry institutions. It as an area of weakness that affects all aspects of Israeli life— and has done so for at least the past three decades, if not longer, as Israeli political scientists have noted on more than one occasion (Akzin and Dror 1966). The great irony, however, is that at least in theory such a problem should not exist at all in Israel, given its traditional socialist ethos and centralized structure. That it does exist is but the final indication that the system has become fatally flawed, if it cannot even do what in principle it should do best.

What is this central defect in Israeli governance? The virtually complete lack of long-term planning in almost all of Israel's ministries (with the notable exception of Defense). Even a brief survey of the deficiencies in this regard would lead us too far afield at this stage. Beyond several works bewailing the problem, it should suffice for our purposes here to note the results of a random survey of 375 of Israel's political, social, and economic elite (Knesset members, judges, high level bureaucrats and army officers, professors, corporate officers, editors and journalists, etc.), conducted by the present author in 1988 and 1989. On the question—"do you think Israel has too much/not enough/just the right amount of public planning?"—fully 78 percent of these leaders responded "not enough," while a miniscule 4 percent answered "too much"!

That Israel has a greater degree of future indeterminacy than most other nations is a truism, but rather beside the point, for such problems of future prognostication are to be found mostly in the realm of foreign policy and national security—not in such bread and butter areas as education, health, etc. For example, it does not call for a great degree of foresight (or planning) to determine that based on the number of first graders today, there will be a need for at least an additional X amount of high school classrooms in eight or nine years. No one at present within the Ministry of Education is involved even in such relatively straightforward extrapolations for planning purposes.

Thus, the development of a rational planning system would go far in avoiding many of the social ills which are behind Israel's grassroots revolt. In health, education, communications, as well as manpower planning related to the court system and police force, any sort of mid- to long-term planning apparatus would enable the service system as a whole to better provide for the basic needs of the Israeli population, and in so doing would ameliorate much of the need for the latter to take matters into their own hands.

Is there an inherent contradiction between recommending a higher level of planning at the same time as calling for less centralization and paternalism? Not at all, for much of this planning could well take place on the municipal plane, with greater citizen input to avoid the paternalism pitfall. In addition, what is needed here is not any Israeli parallel to the discredited Soviet Five Year Plans, but rather the nurturing of a more forward-looking public mentality accompanied by the development of general institutional frameworks in which rational analysis and planning can be undertaken, along with built-in flexibility in order to take account of changing variables (either internal, e.g. changing governments, or external, e.g. increased immigration).

In short, while the previous prescriptions had a heavy political component to them (i.e. reorientation of political power relationships towards the public, within the parties, and vis-a-vis local government), this latter suggestion is more technical (or technocratic) in nature, and does not involve any diminution or change from present Israeli political party power relationships. While "planning" is usually associated with socialist policies, the fact that even under Israel's

Labor regime there was little planning to speak of should assuage the public's fears of any return to what it has recently being fighting against. If Israeli socialism without planning proved to be the worst of all worlds, then perhaps planning without socialism might be the best bet to undo the damage.

13

Loyalty, Voice, and Vex It: A Theory of Alter-Politics

Introduction

This book has kept its main focus on the specifics of Israel's interesting grassroots phenomenon. However, it is a rare country indeed where sociopolitical behavior is so unusual that nothing of broader theoretical scope could be learned from the experience. In this particular instance, Israel may have much to offer anyone interested in larger and more generally applicable political theory.

Until around the time of World War II, political science tended to focus almost exclusively on "institutional" or "traditional" modes of political activity. Legislation, public law, the interrelationship and inner dynamics of the branches of government, and other such similar elements, were the central focii of the discipline. True, political philosophers, theorists, and of course propagandists did all relate to the phenomena of political violence, revolution, etc. However, in the main this area of the field remained a disciplinary backwater, and in most cases when it was addressed at all the perspective was mostly of a situation gone terribly wrong.

As a result of the dramatic increase in unconventional political activity around the globe in the post-World War II era, and due to some methodological factors related to the discipline of political science (Zimmerman 1980, 1), the age of "Political Conflict/Extra-Parliamentary Behavior" was ushered in as a recognized *bona fide* subdiscipline.

While there is very little consensus among researchers as to the reasons that underlie the explosion of such political activity around the world (Gurr 1980, 14), there does seem to be fairly broad consensus that normal/formal political activity and extraparliamentary political activity are but two sides of the same coin. In other words, the activist citizen of a state will almost always first choose the accepted path of political communication through the official channels of government—be they contact with legislators, bureaucrats, government ombudspersons, or even lobbyists. It is when these don't function or are not effective that part of the public begins to consider and utilize more "unconventional" means, e.g. protests, riots, hunger strikes, etc., to bring pressure upon the powers-that-be in order to change the law or official policy.

As noted at the end of chapter 5, Albert O. Hirschman's (1970) seminal thesis propounding a gradation of citizen behavior running from loyalty to voice to exit, attempted to address this dichotomy. In his view, pressure on a political (or economic) system—using either the formal/institutionalized channels for that purpose, or more vocal extraparliamentary forms—is considered "voice," a partial breaking of the citizen's "loyalty" to that system for the purpose of causing it to mend its ways.

This typology does match in a gross sense the two major political science approaches to citizen political activity: "loyal"/normal activity such as voting, lobbying, campaigning (generally called "politics"); and "voice"/extra-parliamentary activity such as protesting, rioting, and the like (termed here for our purposes "extrapolitics"). But what of "exit"? Where is the parallel in the real political world?

Heretofore, political scientists have tended to view "exit" on two planes: the individual and the collective. On the individual level, there exist the widespread phenomena of political alienation, apathy, and/or inactivity; on the collective level, revolution and/or mass emigration are the two major types of political "exit." The former are exclusively passive and introverted—attempts to withdraw psychologically from the political world while physically remaining within the state's territorial jurisdiction. The latter modes are active and extroverted, albeit with the first trying to eliminate the system while the second attempts rather to escape it geographically.

Can there exist something in between, something which combines both withdrawal and undermining, apathy and activism at one and the same time? Interestingly, Hirschman enticingly suggested that this was what he intended to do: "a niche thus exists for this book, which affirms that the choice is often between articulation and 'desertion'—voice and exit" (Hirschman 1970, 31). But it turns out that what he meant was that there is a dynamic interplay between the two choices (true as far as it goes), and not that there may exist some alternative middle ground between voice and exit as he defined them.

The grassroots revolts in Israel suggest that not only can such a thing theoretically exist, but that in fact it exemplifies a rather new approach by disgruntled publics in the contemporary era. Before embarking on a short analysis of the larger theoretical implications of Israel's grassroots phenomenon, though, it would be useful to present some background description of relevant trends in the contemporary world.

Alter-Politics: Origins and Conditions

The general assumption has been that when extrapolitical activity does not work, i.e. is not effective (and of course where normal parliamentary activity long ceased being an effective means of change in any specific country), the solution is to withdraw inwards away from the public realm or emigrate from it altogether, or alternatively to ratchet up the level of antisystem activity in order to topple the regime and substitute something more "responsive" in its place. But these are two quite extreme approaches. On the one hand, after the investment of emotion and energy in extraparliamentary action, many people may find it too difficult to admit defeat or turn into passive subjects of the system. On the other hand, a turn to revolutionary action may be even more psychologically difficult for normally law-abiding citizens—not to mention the huge risk to life, limb, and liberty which few are willing to undertake.

In the past, given the rather limited resources of the general population, not much else could be done. But in the post-industrial era, characterized by relative widespread wealth, knowledge, education, and mass communications, another option presents itself. Let us call it *alter-politics*: bypassing the traditional system of governmental services, and establishing alternative social and economic networks to offer what the official political system cannot, or will not, provide.

In one sense, it is surprising that Hirschman did not consider this possibility, for after all, his analysis relied at least as heavily on economics as it did on political science. The alter-political approach is but a special case of increased competition, albeit here in original fashion by the public against the government. Hirschman does indeed note the importance of *originality* in the voice/exit dynamic, but misses the possibility of alter-politics as an alternative solution:

...in the choice between voice and exit, voice will often lose out, not necessarily because it would be less effective than exit, but because its effectiveness depends on the *discovery* of *new* ways of exerting influence and pressure toward recovery. However 'easy' such a discovery may look in retrospect the chances for it are likely to be heavily discounted in *ex ante* estimates, for creativity always comes as a surprise. Loyalty...thereby pushes men into the alternative, creativity-requiring course of action from which they would normally recoil (Hirschman 1970, 80).

However, there is more to Hirschman's missing the alter-political potential option than simple "discounting" of public creativity. In point of fact, in 1970 there was still very little *alter-politics* in evidence, which is why he (along with political scientists in general) did not relate to it.

The reason lies in the aforementioned resources required for the alter-political "strategy." As was noted in chapter 3, a country's population would need a fairly high level of education in order to know how to set up, and supervise, the alternative system. In addition, unless a large segment of the public had the economic resources to maintain such a system, it would have little chance of success. Moreover, such a network would have to be widespread enough to act as a political bulwark against governmental reprisal, legal or otherwise. Finally, the existence of extensive mass media is an additional requisite for the rapid and effective communication of the development and maintenance of such alternative networks. The media also educate others in the ways of alternative systems, enabling different groups or sectors with their own socioeconomic frustrations to imitate previously proven methods.

None of this is to say that such alter-politics can or will be found everywhere in the contemporary world. If the sufficient condition is postindustrial wealth (in the widest sense of the term), the necessary condition must be a seriously dysfunctional political system which is largely unresponsive to the wishes of the electorate and unmoved by the pressure of extraparliamentary activism.

For obvious reasons, there are as yet not many such countries around. It stands to reason that a system free and open enough to enable the society and economy to reach the postindustrial stage of development, would also be relatively sensitive to political or extrapolitical input. However, precisely the same positive characterisitics of postindustrialism mentioned above may in the future lead to the political system's inability to provide such publicly desired output.

The evidence is there for all to see. For example, the United States—highly educated, and quite wealthy by world standards—has begun to suffer recently from a growing political paralysis borne of political and extrapolitical overload. Whatever the issue, enough well-educated and motivated citizens/groups are willing and able to communicate their wishes and demands to their representatives—either politically ("normal" lobbying) or extrapolitically ("unconventional" pressure). This has led not only to the Congress becoming increasingly fragmented along sectoral and interest-group lines, but also to each legislator finding it very difficult to make a politically "wise" decision. Whatever he decides, significant groups will be alienated and will not forget the "transgression" come next election day. The United States budget approval debacle of October 1990 was merely the clearest example of the increasing legislative fragmentation and paralysis in which a modern "hyperrepresentative" polity can find itself.

But this phenomenon is not merely an outgrowth of the peculiar nature of the American political construct in which federal, regional, and sectoral differences compound the difficulties already inherent in a system of checks and balances. More importantly and significantly, it is due to the complex nature of postindustrial issues as well as the makeup of the postindustrial population (educated, etc.). Barring a total regression from postindustrial economic, educational, and media trends (not at all likely), or a radical change in the representative system as presently constituted around the world, such political paralysis should only get worse in the years to come—forcing the increasingly frustrated publics of the developed world to take matters into their own hands.

This is precisely what the Israelis have done, along a whole host of issue areas as described in part II of this book. In essence, these were clear examples of how an increasingly disgruntled and frustrated democratic citizenry can *vex* the formal system (by establishing alternatives) rather than *exit* (through revolution or emigration).

Preliminary Hypotheses, Political Science Implications

What hypotheses can be generated and lessons learned from the Israeli grassroots revolts? First and foremost, it is clear that there is a direct relationship between alter-politics and politics, despite the fact that the former is an attempt to get away from the clutches of the latter. Indeed, the great irony here is that there may be a greater probability of systemic change in the traditional system as a result of alter-politics than of extrapolitics which more consciously tries to bring about such reform!

The reason for this is that the successful development of alternative service systems by the public strikes at the very heart of the established system's legitimacy (and authority). It is one thing to pressure the government on its own turf, as extra-(parliamentary) politics does; this at least reinforces the government's inherent legitimacy, notwithstanding the demands for change. It is quite another to avoid the authorities altogether, as if they are no longer relevant to the issue at hand. No regime can long endure such "benign neglect"; either it forcefully prevents alter-politics from succeeding (increasingly difficult given the nature of the population it is dealing with, as noted earlier), or it removes the necessity for the alternative system by reforming itself along similar lines.

Thus, the neologism alter-politics has a double meaning. Not only is its original goal the establishment of an *alternative* service system, but its perhaps unintended (although from the practitioners' perspective, wholly salutary) effect is to actually succeed in *altering* the traditional system. Because of this possibility (perhaps probability?) alter-politics cannot be truly considered "exit" in the sense of Hirschman's theory, for the road back to the traditional political authority is a short and easy one (assuming the success of the alter-political effort).

Why is it more than likely that alter-politics will be crowned with at least a modicum of success? As we have seen from the Israeli case, there always exists the possibility that such alternative systems will degenerate into rank illegalism, or that seamy population elements will become heavily involved and enriched. Thus, beyond the threat of direct competition to the official system, the secondary effects can be socially deleterious and have influence far beyond the limited purview of the problematic issue-area at hand. It is to forestall that wider social eventuality that the authorities must respond sooner or later with force or concession.

Beyond this, the Israeli case suggests that the phenomenon of alter-politics may be found equally among democratic and nondemocratic nations, for different reasons. On the democratic side, although there may be less need for such an approach on the one hand because democracy is generally more responsive to politics and extrapolitics, on the other hand the resources of the population will be greater as a rule, enabling them more easily to establish such alternative systems. Second, democratic law usually works under the assumption that anything not expressly prohibited is permitted; this allows for greater latitude by the disgruntled population to find the "holes" in the law for alter-political purposes.

Nondemocracies are more governmentally coercive and more legally restrictive—but overall also less successful in providing the services (or productive economic environment) which the public craves. Moreover, some autocratic regimes—especially those without undue socioeconomic ideological baggage—may actually secretly welcome a measure of alter-politics which can serve to produce some of the output the established system is incapable of providing.

Where, then, are other examples of alter-politics? To give but two examples, from opposite sides of the democratic divide: in the United States—speakeasies during Prohibition, all-white private schools during desegregation, underground abortion clinics in states with restrictive legislation, home education for children; in *pre-glasnost* Poland—private farm plots (an unusual preindustrial, and not postindustrial, case).

What are the practical implications for political science? First, to recognize the existence of these quasi-institutions and to determine the extent to which this general phenomenon is prevalent around the world. Second, to understand that such public activity is not merely socioeconomic in character but at base quite political as well. In other words, we should be exploring the reasons for the development of alter-politics in various nations through the prism of political dysfunction. One of the more interesting questions is whether there exists some "universal law" whereby alter-politics appears only after political and extrapolitical means were attempted by the public and failed. It may well be (especially in nondemocracies) that the extrapolitical stage is skipped over, for fairly obvious reasons.

A third question is whether indeed a certain level of socioeconomic advancement is a necessary condition for the appearance of alter-politics, or whether in certain circumstances (e.g. Polish farmers) even a backward segment of a relatively underdeveloped country may get successfully involved in such activity.

Fourth and finally, it would be worthwhile to test the hypothesis that alter-politics may be more successful than extrapolitics in fomenting systemic change within the regime. That this was largely the case in Israel does not mean that it is true everywhere. Vexing the government authorities through alter-political service networks may not guarantee that they will feel an imperative to change the way they run their own service system.

In the final analysis, there seems to be little doubt that a broad ground exists in the polity between failed voice and final exit. It is a nebulous area, heretofore bereft of scholarly effort—even of much academic notice. If postindustrial Israel is anything to go on, the discipline would do well to start paying some attention to this research *tabula rasa*.

14

Between Past and Future: Israel's Grassroots Revolts in Historical Cross-Comparative Perspective

Revolt at Forty: The American Precedent

As was argued in the previous chapter in general theoretical terms, and as has been mentioned in passing several times throughout this book, Israel's grassroots revolts have parallels elsewhere—in their causal factors and general spirit, if not the actual specifics of their local expression. Even this is not going far enough, for there exist broader historical comparisons which can shed further light on Israel's "wildfire" phenomenon. The reverse is true as well: a cross-comparative analysis could show that the Israeli condition has much to teach others undergoing a similar experience.

This first section will look at the American parallel, not only because the United States has had the most influence on Israel's grassroots revolts (e.g. Black Panthers, Reaganism, Project Renewal), but because it developed historically in remarkably similar fashion from the perspective of our subject. However, the following highly schematic discussion is not meant to suggest any iron law of developmental history or even an exact identity between the American and Israeli historical experiences, but rather to show that what is happening in Israel of late is not altogether new, and to reemphasize once again that it may not even be as "dangerous" as one might suppose at first glance. In short, such a brief comparison with the United States might at the least offer some solace and even hope for Israel's future in this regard.

Not coincidentally, both the United States and Israel underwent a process of grassroots revolt around the fourth decade of their constitutional development. The American equivalent, of course, was what came to be known as the Jacksonian Era, or America's "second democratic revolution."

Why specifically and uncoincidentally after forty years? The Bible itself presents an answer of sorts: it takes approximately that long for the elder founding generation to pass from the scene. The Children of Israel would not be ready for the rigors of the Promised Land until all who were socialized in Pharaoh's centralized and over-bearing Egypt had passed away. Only those who were never slaves, who had not been led (much against their will) out of Egypt by a strong leader, would have enough personal initiative to run their own society, would be "free men" in the active sense and not merely in the technical sense of not being formally shackled.

Thus, just as happened in Israel (if one permits for the sake of illustration the chronologically backwards analogy), the Jacksonian Revolution occurred only after the founding fathers had left the scene—indeed, both John Adams and Thomas Jefferson died on July 4, 1826 (exactly fifty years to the day from the signing of the Declaration of Independence!), two years prior to Andrew Jackson's election. In both national cases, a new generation was coming into its own—one no longer overawed by the shadow of the country's founding fore-bears, and only too eager to assert itself in a more free-spirited fashion.

Many of the same unruly social phenomena found in Israel circa the 1980s were in evidence in America of the 1820s as well, spear-headed by a populist government not unlike the Likud. This was a revolt against the Eastern establishment (America's version of Mapai), as Jackson became the first president elected from, and repre-senting, the "periphery" (i.e. west of the Appalachians), just as the Likud drew heavy sustenance from the development towns.

Nor was this merely a geographical revolt; Jackson campaigned against "bargain and corruption"—the 1824 backroom political deal-ings in the Congress that kept the presidency in the hands of the political establishment (despite the fact that Jackson had garnered a plurality of popular and electoral votes). One needs hardly mention that the Likud came to power as a revolt against the scandals and clubbiness of the Mapai old-boy's network. Even the campaign style was similar and symbolic of the new era: Jackson was the first presi-dential candidate to be elected by a direct appeal to the masses rather than through the support of a well-oiled party bureaucracy—precise-ly the way Menachem Begin brought his party to power.

Not the least remarkable triumph of the Jackson campaign was its success in picturing the candidate as the embodiment of democra-cy, despite the fact that he had espoused conservative positions for over thirty years, e.g. vigorously opposing legislative relief of debtors. Begin and the Likud too were the economically conservative party (in the traditional laissez faire sense of economic conservatism), and yet managed to draw their greatest support from the workers and down-trodden as a protest vote against perceived privilege. While Jackson's opponents Clay and Adams stood for greater national economic planning, he demanded decentralized economic policies—despite the potential hardship it could bring to his lower class supporters. In the event, in an amazing augury of Israeli things to come Jackson's policies did lead to the panic and depression of 1837—much the same way the Likud's policies caused the economic debacle of the early 1980s!

Moreover, it was precisely Jackson's not having served any long apprenticeship in government (and despite not having any real experience in the formulation and conduct of foreign policy), which was viewed as a plus by the voters increasingly fed up with the imperiousness of the Republican party brahmans. In parallel fashion, the Likud's relative governmental inexperience stood it in good stead from the perspective of an Israeli public increasingly disgusted with experienced politics as practiced in the 1970s. This also explains why Jackson's declared use of the "spoils system" (placing his own men within the bureaucracy) was viewed with unjaundiced aplomb by the American public—much as was the case in Israel when the Likud attempted to rotate out the entrenched Mapai bureaucrats.

Such a grassroots political upheaval is almost inevitably met by scurrilous attacks, because of its very "low-class" nature. If the *edot ha'mizrakh* were called contemptuous names and Begin himself suffered the poisoned slings of his opponents who took pains to remind one and all of his terrorist background (not that he wasn't himself a pro at political attack), this was but an eerie echo of the portrayal of Jackson as a barbarian who was "covered with the blood of Indians."

In short, virtually all the same unseemly and problematic elements of Israel's grassroots political antiestablishmentism were to be found a century and a half earlier in the United States. And as is common knowledge, not only did America get through that tumultuous period, but it set the stage for a demographic and economic growth virtually unparalleled in the world at that time, once the democratic revolution had taken root. Those who look askance upon the contemporary phenomenon in Israel, might do well to heed the following *Encyclopedia Americana* (1989, 15:646) description and analysis of the Jacksonian Era in historical hindsight:

Historians have debated the significance of Jacksonian Democracy for many decades. Those of the nineteenth century emphasized mob vulgarity and the spoils system as its hallmarks, only

to yield to...the Progressive Era, who saw Jackson and his policies as the reflecton of the frontier spirit, which they considered
the essence of American democracy.... Modern study...saw
Jacksonians as...would be entrepeneurs anxious to dismantle
existing vested interests....

Few today look back upon the years 1828–1836 as a period of acute danger to American democracy but rather as the first irruption and expression of the latent talents, which underlay the system from the start.

Much the same can be said for Israel. It has always been a great
paradox—and source of no little consternation to its friends around
the world—how a country of Jews, a people ostensibly blessed with
the greatest intellectual, political, and especially economic acumen,
could have developed a system of such byzantine and stultifying proportions. This is not to deny that Israel's founding generation must
also be credited with leading the country at a time of almost unparalleled growth during the years 1954–1973; we have noted the circumstances which pushed them into a centralistic and paternalistic governing philosophy, useful at the time. There can equally be no denying that such a system has long passed its utility and only hinders the
still tremendous potential of its talented population.

Not unlike the Jacksonian Revolution, then, Israel's contemporary grassroots revolts should be understood for what they really represent: a population too long chafing at the bit to show what it really
could accomplish if it were left mostly to its own devices. Indeed,
most of the alternative systems which were outlined in this book have
proven to be pretty successful (e.g. grey education, private health)—
and this while working against the wishes of the government. It can
well be imagined what could be accomplished were the public's
efforts channeled in a fashion complementary, and not in opposition,
to the ruling authorities.

Returning to the Source: Eastern Europe and the Israeli Experience

If Israel's grassroots revolt followed the early United States
model, and drew some direct inspiration from more contemporary
American developments, could Israel serve as an object lesson for
others undergoing a similar process? Here, too, the answer is yes. The
most dramatic development in the world of the late 1980s and early
1990s has been the Soviet and East European revolutionary turn away
from the communist totalitarian model of government (once again,
approximately forty years after the Soviets established their totalitari-

an regime in those enslaved countries). What is interesting here, despite the obvious qualitative difference between communist totalitarianism and Israel's much milder form of traditional quasi-authoritarian socialism, is the fact (already hinted at in chapter 2) that all the elements found in Israel's grassroots revolts—antipaternalism, anticentralism, and antisocialism—are in evidence as well in the East European case, only more so.

Indeed, as Sharkansky (1987, 5) has noted, "it is Israel's fate to suffer the worst from the centrally controlled East and the democratic West." As we saw in chapter 1, the Israeli politico-economic system was modeled on the Central European approach in the early twentieth century, and the entire grassroots revolt phenomenon of late is in a sense a Western European/American-style reaction to that type of system. Israel's grassroots revolts, then, have been public battles for the social, economic, and political soul of the country—well before the historic events of the late eighties in Eastern Europe. Notwithstanding certain obvious differences, it can still serve, therefore, as an object lesson for that part of the world.

What are the lessons to be learned here? First of all, it is not necessarily the most impoverished countries of the world which may find themselves in the throes of public antipaternalistic pressure and revolt. If the Israeli case is anything to go by, then one may posit that the more economically advanced the socialist society, the greater the libertarian urge on the part of the increasingly mature citizenry. This is not merely a matter of economic self-interest (greater personal control of disposable income), but of psychological sociopolitical desire. Such societies invariably do succeed in raising the general population's educational level, and concomitantly there emerges the need for personal expression through, and beyond, economic gratification.

This is in essence Abraham Maslow's graduated scale of self-actualization extrapolated to the public at large (Maslow 1954, 80–92). Once a certain level of economic sufficiency is reached, personal self-expression becomes the next human goal. In that sense, paternalistic and collectivist societies are by their very nature self-destructive. The more they succeed in raising the population's standard of living (assuming that they manage to succeed at all; if they don't, they suffer even worse problems), the more that population feels a lack of psychological quality of life.

But as the Israeli case shows, such a revolt must emerge from the grassroots. Here the lesson bifurcates in the Eastern European case. In all of the Soviet satellites, the revolution came from the people, and can be said to have been genuinely populistic as well as popular. While the ultimate success of each of these countries is dependent in some measure on their current economic situation, no less important is the relative grassroots experience, which each had before the actual events of 1989 (East Germany is an exception to the rule, for obvious reasons). Poland, Hungary, and to a lesser extent Czechoslovakia, had made previous attempts in the past to attain, and/or were afforded a degree of, social freedom. This should stand them in good stead as compared to Bulgaria and Romania which start their grassroots revolutions virtually from scratch.

The Soviet Union, on the other hand, cannot be said to have undergone a grassroots revolution (except perhaps in the Baltic and Southern Moslem republics), but rather paradoxically a paternalistic "democratic revolution" from on high. Here the dismantling of the centralized system has been initiated by the central authorities themselves; freedom has been "granted" by the benevolent paterfamilias Mr. Gorbachev. It is unlikely that the Russian people are truly ready for a grassroots revolution if the citizens weren't the ones to initiate it or even are able to fully appreciate something which they hadn't fought for but rather were presented with (on a tin platter, so to speak).

Put another way, grassroots revolutions do not erupt *sui generis*, but are the product of a percolation process usually of several decades duration. If it took Israeli society close to four decades to mature and grow out of its paternalistic cocoon, then one cannot expect the Soviet people to know overnight how best to exploit their newfound freedom without having undergone similar gestation pangs. Eastern Europe, on the other hand, follows more closely the Israeli model and thus its democratic future is more secure, although by no means guaranteed.

Beyond this, a second major lesson can be gleaned from the Israeli experience, and it bears directly on the nature and manifestations of the grassroots revolt itself. Once the public begins to breathe the air of personal freedom, such liberty cannot be readily compartmentalized into a few specific areas of the government's choosing. While Israel's grassroots revolt may have commenced in the political sphere (i.e. mass demonstrations), it soon carried over to the economic realm and from there to education, health, leisure, religion, etc. In short, such grassroots revolts are hardly ever unidimensional because the underlying grievance is not against the malfunctioning of any specific area of national life but rather versus that governing philosophy, which won't let the citizenry run their lives across the board.

In this respect, at least, Gorbachev was correct in combining political *glasnost* with economic *perestroika*. He understood not only that it was futile to advance one area of society without a commensurate step forward in others, but that once any single area was "opened up," the public would not stand for the continuation of centralized paternalism in the others. His problem, though, is that it is much easier to advance political *glasnost* than economic *perestroika;* the ever-widening gap between the two is itself a danger to the entire enterprise.

Conversely, the Communist Chinese rulers did not really grasp the underlying truism here. The post-Mao leadership believed that economic freedom could be dispensed in measured doses without any parallel change occurring in the political field. The events there in 1989, especially the Tianamin Square massacre, are belated recognition of that error, although in the Chinese case the immediate response was an attempt to stem the grassroots tide by turning back the clock. Once opened, however, the grassroots Pandora's box cannot ever really be hermetically sealed again.

A third and final lesson that can be adduced from Israel's grassroots revolts is the almost inevitable social price which must be paid with the dismantling of socialism and overweaning government control. As we have witnessed in a number of different Israeli areas of life—pirate cable television, black medicine, the underground economy—there seems to be no avoiding a certain increase in quasi-illegal (at times, outright criminal) behavior, at least over the short term.[1] There are a couple of reasons for this.

On the one hand, in any radical changeover from (or indirect attack against) a stultified, centralized system, in favor of an open,

---

[1] *Ha'aretz* (8/24/90, 1c) reported a true anecdote which exemplifies this problem. MK Pessah Grupper, a member of the Knesset's Finance Committee, had to make an upcoming decision regarding a change in the system of grants given to all new immigrants. Traditionally, each immigrant family was given significant sales and purchase tax reductions for one of each household appliance on an approved list (including a car). The draft bill on the committee's agenda would switch this to one overall large financial grant, and abolish the lower tax rights.

One day, while in a household appliance store in Haifa, he was approached by two Russian *olim* who asked if he was interested in purchasing a new appliance "very cheap." With some prodding, he discovered that they had no need for a certain appliance, but did not wish to "waste" their tax right. So they were offering to purchase the item with their rights, and split the savings between him and themselves! MK Grupper immediately made up his mind as to his future committee vote. Beyond this, though, here is an example of the ability of even "greenhorn" capitalists to exploit the paternalistic distortions of a centralized (albeit benevolent) system in the furtherance of free personal choice.

multichoice one, institutional asymmetries will inevitably exist. While the popular demand or expectation may be for freedom across the board, as was just noted the reality of development in certain social realms of endeavor will inevitably lag somewhat behind the others. It is within these "retarded" pockets that segments of the public may take things into their own hands to speed the process along, in order to bring them up to the more developed areas in society. By definition, a lot of such "expediting" will involve antinormative, if not outright illegal, activity (*Business Week* 6/5/89, 66, 70).

On the other hand, there will always be those who are incapable of handling such freedom in the way that it was meant. Give some children $100 in a candy store and they will most likely take as much (or even more) than they can carry or eat. Remove overbearing governmental strictures "overnight," and some adults will have trouble differentiating between freedom and license. This is not so much the price of undue liberty as it is of overdue liberation. Freedom takes a little getting used to, but this minor problem is surely worth the ultimate goal of a socially unfettered life—and certainly not enough justification for condemning outright the larger grassroots phenomenon.

In the final analysis, then, the really important aspect of Israel's dismantling of socialism and freeing itself from the paternalistic yoke—similar to processes occurring in most of Eastern Europe—is not that the well-educated policymakers have become aware of their system's economic and philosophical bankruptcy, but rather that the "less sophisticated" citizenry are the source that pushed their country in that direction. In a situation where the dramatic changes spring from the populace, there is all the chance in the world that the new system coming into being will be successful and ultimately lead to sociopolitical stability—once the not inconsiderable transitional difficulties and seemier elements are overcome and left behind.

Wildfire Revisited

In the end, Israel's grassroots revolt turns out indeed to be "wildfire"—in the original sense of the word. This is not a searing phenomenon which threatens to leave behind it scorched earth but rather a trailblazing venture into the unknown. Like Prometheus stealing the heavenly fire for the benefit of mankind, Israelis, too, are seeking the path to personal freedom and social liberation in order to most fully actualize their burning potentialities. It is a risky affair, even revolting at times. But can one deny the most fundamental human drive underlying its expression?

Bibliography

Books and Journal Articles

Akzin, Benjamin, and Dror, Yehezkel (1966). *Israel: High Pressure Planning*. Syracuse, NY: Syracuse University Press.

Al-Haj, Majid, and Rosenfeld, Henry (1990). *Arab Local Government in Israel*. Boulder, CO: Westview Press.

Aran, Gideon (1985). *Eretz Yisrael Bein Dat U'politikah: Ha'tenuah Le'atzirat Ha'nesigah Be'Sinai U'lekakhehah* [The Land of Israel Between Politics and Religion: The Movement to Stop the Withdrawal from Sinai and the Lessons to be Learned]. Jerusalem: The Jerusalem Institute for Israel Studies.

Arian, Alan (1968). *Ideological Change in Israel*. Cleveland: Case Western Reserve University Press.

———. (1985). *Politics in Israel: The Second Generation*. Chatham, NJ: Chatham House Publishers.

Avi-hai, Avraham (1974). *Ben-Gurion, State Builder: Principles and Pragmatism, 1948–1963*. New York: John Wiley and Sons.

Bank of Israel (1986). *Din Ve'kheshbon Lishnat 1985* [1985 Annual Report]. Jerusalem: Government Printing Office.

———. (1990). *Din Ve'kheshbon Lishnat 1989* [1989 Annual Report]. Jerusalem: Government Printing Office.

Bar-On, Mordechai (1985). *Shalom Akh'shav: Le'diyuknah Shel Te'nuah* [Peace Now: Portrait of a Movement]. Tel Aviv: Hakibbutz Hameukhad.

Bar Siman-Tov, Ronit (1989). *Tokhnit Limudim No'sefet Be'mimun Ha'horim: Seker Rishoni* [Extra-curricular Studies Paid for by Parents: A First Survey]. Jerusalem: Henrietta Szold Institute.

Bar-Zohar, Michael (1978). *Ben-Gurion*, transl. by Peretz Kidron. London: Weidenfeld and Nicolson.

Ben-Yehuda, Nachman (1989). "The Social Meaning of Alternative Systems: Some Exploratory Notes," in *The Israeli State and Society: Boundaries and Frontiers*, ed. Baruch Kimmerling. Albany, NY: SUNY Press, pp.152–164.

———. (1990). *The Politics and Morality of Deviance*. Albany, NY: State University of New York Press.

Blasi, Joseph (1986). *The Communal Experience of the Kibbutz*. New Brunswick, NJ: Transaction Books.

Caspi, Dan (1986). *Media Decentralization: The Case of Israel's Local Newspapers*. New Brunswick: Transaction Books.

Cohen, Erik (1972). "The Black Panthers in Israeli Society," *Jewish Journal of Sociology*, vol. 14, #1 (June), pp.93–110.

Cohen, Mitchell (1987). *Zion and State: Nation, Class and the Shaping of Modern Israel*. Oxford: Basil Blackwell.

Cromer, Gerald (1976). "The Israeli Black Panthers: Fighting for Credibility and a Cause," *Victimology: An International Journal*, vol. 1, #3 (Fall), pp.403–413.

Danet, Brenda (1988). *Pulling Strings: Biculturalism in Israeli Bureaucracy*. Albany, NY: State University of New York Press.

Don-Yehiya, Eliezer (1977). *Shituf Ve'konflikt Bain Makhanot Politiyyim: Ha'makhaneh Ha'dati U'tenuat Ha'avodah U'mashbair Ha'khinukh Be'Yisrael* [Cooperation and Conflict Between Political Camps: The Religious Camp and the Labor Movement and the Education Crisis in Israel]. Jerusalem: Doctoral Dissertation presented to the Department of Political Science, Hebrew University, 3 vols.

Efrat, Elisha (1988). *Geography and Politics in Israel Since 1967*. London: Frank Cass.

Elazar, Daniel J. (1981). "The Kehilla: From its Beginnings to the End of the Modern Epoch," in *Comparative Jewish Politics: Public Life in Israel and the Diaspora*, Sam Lehman-Wilzig & Bernard Susser, eds. Ramat Gan: Bar-Ilan University Press, pp.23–63.

———. (1988). "The Local Dimension in Israeli Government and Politics," in *Local Government in Israel*, eds. Daniel Elazar & Chaim Kalcheim. Lanham, MD: University Press of America; The Jerusalem Center for Public Affairs/Center for Jewish Community Studies, pp.3–40.

Ellenczweig, Avi Yacar. (1983). "The New Israeli Health Care Reform: An Analysis of a National Need," *Journal of Health Politics, Policy and Law*, vol. 8, #2 (Summer), pp.366–386.

Encyclopedia Americana, ed. David Holland (1989). "Andrew Jackson." Danbury, CT: Grolier, Inc., vol. 15., p.646.

Etzioni-Halevy, Eva (1975). "Protest Politics in the Israeli Democracy," *Political Science Quarterly*, vol. 90, #3 (Fall), pp.497–520.

Gary, Dorit Phyllis (1984). "Letter From Israel," *Columbia Journalism Review*, vol. 23, #4 (Nov.–Dec. 1984), pp.48–52.

Gottlieb, Avi & Yuchtman-Yaar, Ephraim (1985). "Materialism, Postmaterialism, and Public Views on Socioeconomic Policy: the Case of Israel," in *Politics and Society in Israel: Studies of Israeli Society, vol. III*, ed. Ernest Krausz. New Brunswick: Transaction Books, pp.385–412.

Gurr, Ted Robert (1980). *Handbook of Political Conflict: Theory and Research.* New York: The Free Press.

Halper, Jeff, *et al.* (1989). "Communities, Schools, and Integration," in *Education in a Comparative Context: Studies of Israeli Society: Volume IV*, ed. Ernest Krausz. New Brunswick, NJ: Transaction Books, pp.269–284.

Hasson, Shlomo (1987). *Mekha'at Ha'dor Ha'sheni: Te'nuot Ironiyyot-Khevratiyyot Bi'Yerushalayyim* [The Protest of the Second Generation: Urban Social Movements in Jerusalem]. Jerusalem: Institute for Israeli Studies.

Hirschman, Albert O. (1970). *Exit, Voice and Loyalty: Responses to Declines in Firms, Organizations, and States.* Cambridge, MA: Harvard University Press.

I.M.F. Yearbook 1983 (1983). Washington: International Monetary Fund.

Kimmerling, Baruch (1983). *Zionism and Economy.* Cambridge, Mass.: Schenkman Publishing Co.

King, Paul, *et al.* (1987). *Project Renewal in Israel: Urban Revitalization Through Partnership.* Lanham, MD: University Press of America; The Jerusalem Center for Public Affairs/Center for Jewish Community Studies.

Kleinberger, Aharon (1969). *Society, Schools, and Progress in Israel.* Oxford: Pergamon Press, 1969.

Landau, Jacob (1969). *The Arabs in Israel: A Political Study.* London: Oxford University Press.

Lehman-Wilzig, Sam (1982). "Public Protests against Central and Local Government in Israel, 1950–1979," *The Jewish Journal of Sociology*, vol. 24, #2 (December), pp.99–115.

———. (1988). "Turning Point," *Present Tense*, March/April, pp.15–19.

———. (1989). "Israel: Red is Dead," *Midstream*, vol. 35, #8 (November), pp. 9–12.

———. (1990a). "Israel's Grassroots Libertarian Revolution," *The Freeman*, April, pp.144–148.

———. (1990b). *Stiff-Necked People, Bottle-Necked System: The Evolution and*

Roots of Israeli Public Protest, 1949–1986. Bloomington, IN: Indiana University Press.

————. (1991). "*Am K'shei Oref*: Oppositionism in the Jewish Heritage," *Judaism*, vol. 40, #1 (Winter), pp.16–38.

Levitan, Dov (1983). "*Aliyat Marvad Ha'kesamim Ke'hemshaikh Histori Le'aliyot Mi'Taiman May'az TRM"B: Nituakh Socio-Politi Shel Aliyatam U'Klitatam Shel Yehudai Taiman Be'Yisrael Be'ait Ha'khadasha*" [Operation Magic Carpet as an Historical Continuation of Jewish Emigration From Yemen Since 1882: A Socio-Political Analysis of the Immigration and Absorption of the Yemenite Jews in Israel in Modern Times]. Ramat Gan: Master's Thesis presented to the Department of Political Studies, Bar-Ilan Univerity, Israel.

Liebman, Charles (1988). "Conceptions of the 'State of Israel' in Israeli Society," *The Jerusalem Quarterly*, Number 47 (Summer), pp.95–107.

Liebman, Charles, and Don-Yehiya, Eliezer (1983). *Civil Religion in Israel: Traditional Religion and Political Culture in the Jewish State*. Berkeley: University of California Press.

————. (1984). *Religion and Politics in Israel*. Bloomington, IN: Indiana University Press.

Lustick, Ian (1980). *Arabs in the Jewish State: Israel's Control of a National Minority*. Austin: University of Texas Press.

Marcus, Gad (1989). "*Zekhuyot Hatzba'ah Le'minayot*" [Stock Voting Rights]. *Nihul*, June, p.51.

Maslow, Abraham (1954). *Motivation and Personality*. New York: Harper and Row.

Migdal, Joel (1989). "The Crystallization of the State and the Struggles Over Rulemaking: Israel in Comparative Perspective," in *The Israeli State and Society: Boundaries and Frontiers*, ed. Baruch Kimmerling. Albany: State University of New York Press.

Peled, Israel (1988). "Legal Structure of the Local Authority," in *Local Government in Israel*, eds. Daniel Elazar & Chaim Kalcheim. Lanham, MD: University Press of America; The Jerusalem Center for Public Affairs/Center for Jewish Community Studies, pp.165–197.

Peri, Yoram (1989). "Less Democracy or More?" *Israeli Democracy*, Fall, pp.4–6.

Perlman, Janice E. (1979). "Grassrooting the System," in *Strategies of Community Organization, 3rd edition*, Fred M. Cox et al., eds. Itasca, IL: F.E. Peacock, pp.403–425.

Ra'anan, Zvi (1981). *Gush Emunim* [The Bloc of the Faithful]. Tel Aviv: Sifriat Poalim.

Rabushka, Alvin, & Hanke, Steve H. (1989). *Likrat Tzmikha: Tokhnit Lit'khiya Kalkalit Be'Yisrael* [Towards Growth: A Blueprint for Economic Rebirth in Israel]. Jerusalem: Institute for Advanced Strategic and Political Studies.

Rabushka, Alvin (1990a). *Te'udat Tziyunim La'meshek Ha'Yisraeli: Skirah Lishnat 1989* [Report Card for the Israeli Economy: Survey for 1989]. Jerusalem: Institute for Advanced Strategic and Political Studies.

_____ (1990b). *Arikha May'khadash Shel Sidrei-Ha'adifuyyot: Skirah Bikoratit Shel Takziv Medinat Yisrael Lishnat 1990* [Reordering Priorities: A Critical Survey of Israel's 1990 Budget]. Jerusalem: Institute for Advanced Strategic and Political Studies.

Rackman, Emanuel (1955). *Israel's Emerging Constitution, 1948–1951.* New York: Columbia University Press.

Rekhess, Eli (1989). *"Ha'aravim Be'Yisrael Ve'arviyay Ha'shtakhim: Zikah Politit Ve'solidariyut Le'umit, 1967–1988"* [The Arabs in Israel and the Arabs in the Territories: Political Ties and National Solidarity, 1967–1988], in *Ha'mizrakh Heh'khadash*, vol. 32, Nos. 125–128, pp.165–191.

———. (1990). "Arabs in a Jewish State: Images vs. Realities," *Middle East Insight*, January/February, pp.3–9.

Shamir, Michal, & Arian, Asher (1983). "The Ethnic Vote in Israel's 1981 Elections," *The Elections in Israel—1981*. Tel Aviv: Ramot Publishing, pp.91–111.

Shapira, Anita (1985). *May'piturei Ha'ramah ad Peiruk Ha'Palmakh: Sug'yot Bama'avak Al Ha'hanhagah Ha'bitkhonit* [The Army Controversy, 1948: Ben Gurion's Struggle for Control]. Tel Aviv: Ha'kibbutz Hameukhad.

Shapira, Yonathan (1986). *The Formative Years of the Israeli Labor Party.* Beverly Hills: Sage.

Sharkansky, Ira (1987). *The Political Economy of Israel.* New Brunswick, NJ: Transaction Books.

Sprinzak, Ehud (1986). *Eesh Ha'yashar Be'aynav: Ee-legalism Ba'khevrah Ha'yisraelit* [Every Man Whatsoever Is Right in His Own Eyes: Illegalism in Israeli Society]. Tel Aviv: Sifriat Ha'Poalim.

Steinberg, Gerald (1989). *"Mikh'sholim Ba'derekh Le'shinui Mivneh Ma'arekhet Ha'briyut Be'Yisrael"* [Obstacles on the Way to Structural Changes in Israel's Health System], *Bitakhon Soziali*, No. 34, December, pp.61–78.

Susser, Bernard (1989). "'Parliadential' Politics: A Proposed Constitution for Israel," *Parliamentary Affairs*, vol. 42, #1 (January), pp.112–122.

Susser, Bernard & Don-Yehiya, Eliezer (1989). "The Nation v. the People: Israel and the Decline of the Nation State," *Midstream,* vol. 35, #8, November, pp.13–16.

Susser, Bernard & Schreiber, Jacob (1988). "We the Israeli People: A Draft Constitution for Israel," *Midstream,* vol. 34, #6, August–September, pp.13–16.

Tanzi, Vito (1984). *"Ha'sibot Ve'hatotzaot Shel Ha'tofa'ah Ba'olam"* [The Reasons and the Results of the Phenomenon in the World], *Riv'on Le'kalkalah,* No. 122, October, pp.323–328.

Weisburd, David (1989). *Jewish Settler Violence: Deviance as Social Reaction.* University Park, PA: The Pennsylvania State University Press.

Wolffsohn, Michael (1987). *Israel: Polity, Society and Economy, 1882–1986.* Atlantic Highlands, NJ: Humanities Press International.

Yishai, Yael (1987). *Kevutzot Interess Be'Yisrael: Mivkhanah Shel Demokratiah* [Interest Groups in Israel: The Test of Democracy]. Tel Aviv: Am Oved.

Yuchtman-Ya'ar, Ephraim (1989). "Who Do You Trust? The Israeli Public and Its Institutions," *Israel Democracy,* Fall, pp.7–11.

Zilberfarb, Ben-Zion (1984). *"Omdanay Ha'kalkalah Ha'shekhorah Be'Yisrael U'bekhul"* [Estimates of the Black Economy in Israel and Overseas], *Riv'on Le'kalkalah,* No. 122, October, pp.319–322.

Zimmerman, Ekkart (1980). *Political Violence, Crises, and Revolutions: Theories and Research.* Cambridge, MA: Schenkman Publishing.

Newspaper and Magazine Articles

A) *Ha'aretz:*

10/23/87 - The New Conscientious Objectors," Tom Segev, p.5b.

4/28/89 - "Ultra-Orthodox and Secularists: The Bottom Line at Present (Part B)," Boaz Shapira, p.2b.

5/26/89 - "The Leadership of 'the State of Judah' Decided to 'Convene a Military Forum Which Will Establish an Army Infrastructure'," Nadav Shragai, p.5a.

7/30/89 - "Eight 'State of Judah' Activists Were Arrested on Suspicion of Rebellion and Illegal Organization; Most Released," Reuven Shapira [International Edition].

10/27/89 - "The Lost Honor of the Patient," Esther Belaveh, p.6 [International Edition].

1/12/90 - "Arrested State of Judah Organizers Are Interrogated About the Arson of Grapholite [Publishing] and the Sikarikim Affair," Reuven Shapira and Lili Galilee, p.3 [International Edition].

1/26/90 - "*Khasamba* or a New Military Organization?" Yehoshua Meiri, pp.4–7; 47 [Weekend Magazine].

2/9/90 - "I've Lost My Sense of Justice," Ze'ev Schiff, p.3b.

3/9/90a - "Parents Complain About Exploitation of their Holy Studies Moneys for Other Purposes," Nili Mandler & Yehudit Greenblat, p.3 [International Edition].

3/9/90b - "Weaving Economic Dreams," Uriel Ben-Chanan, p.7b [International Edition].

3/9/90c - "The Private Initiative of the '90 Immigrants," Ina Shapiro, p.7b [International Edition].

3/9/90d - "Filled to Capacity," Yehudah Korn, pp.33–38 [Weekend Magazine].

3/9/90e - "Investors Who Set Up Haifa Private Hospital Will Sue [Israeli] Government in South African Court," Edna Aridor, p.4 [International. Edition].

3/16/90 - "A Private Medical Center Inaugurated in Ramat Aviv," Edna Aridor, p.4 [International Edition].

3/23/90a - "Entrance Forbidden to the Sephardim," Yehudit Greenblat, p.4b [International Edition].

3/23/90b - "They Even Deserve It," Ran Kislev, p.8 [International Edition].

3/30/90 - "The Rejected," Iris Milner, p.22; 47 [Weekend Magazine].

4/6/90a - "The Future of the Extreme Right," Nadav Shragai, p. 3b [International Edition].

4/6/90b - "An Israeli Dream," Yisrael Amrani, p.4b [International Edition].

4/8/90 - "'Enough, Disgusting Corrupt Politicians' Charged Posters in the Protest to Change the Election System," Yerakh Tal, p.1.

4/9/90a - "The Framers of the Four Drafts to Change the Election System: In the Future We Shall Unify them into One Bill," Yehudit Greenblat, p.2a.

4/9/90b - "Four Suggestions for Direct Election of the Prime Minister," Amos Ben-Vered, p.2a.

4/9/90c - "How to Reform the Election System," Main Editorial, p.1b.

4/29/90a - "Harish Did Not Find 'Medinat Yehuda' Activity to have Broken the Law and Will Not Prosecute," Gideon Alon, p.2.

4/29/90b - "Petition for Changing the System of Government Will be Handed to the President During the Holiday," n.a., p.1.

5/29/90a - "The Rate of Abortions in Private Hospitals: 66% of the Overall Number," Edna Aridor, p.3a.

5/29/90b - "The Knesset Approved the First Reading of the Draft Bill for Direct Elections of the Prime Minister," Amos Ben-Vered, p.3a.

8/24/90 - "First Lesson in Citizenship," Nechemia Stressler, p.1c.

10/12/90 - "On the Road to a Salary Slip on the Kibbutz," Yossi Melman, p.4b.

10/19/90 - "Labor's Central Committee Ratified the Changeover to a Primaries System and Charging Membership Payments," Yerakh Tal, p.5a.

B) *The Jerusalem Post:*

9/7/83 - "The limits of discipline," Marsha Pomerantz, pp.10–11 [Weekend Magazine].

11/27/87a - "What is ailing Kupat Holim? The political connection," Sarah Honig, p.5.

11/27/87b - "What is ailing Kupat Holim? The professor's prescription," Judy Siegel-Itzkovitch, p.5.

6/8/89 - "Haredim who identify with the state," Joel Rebibo, p.10.

7/14/89 - "A Mediterranean Ruhr," Michael Eilan, pp.4–5 [Weekend Magazine].

8/24/90a - "Recommendation for reforming the health system: Scrap it, start anew," Judy Siegel-Itzkovitch, p.9.

8/24/90b - "Histadrut counterattacks on health-care reform issue," Jacob Wirtschafter, p.18.

9/26/90 - "Bezek stock offer is a bell-ringer," Galit Lipkis, p.6.

9/28/90a - "Peres vies to keep Labor symbols," Michal Yudelman and Sara Honig, p.2.

9/28/90b - "Kessar scores MKs' Histadrut plan," Evelyn Gordon, p.2.

9/28/90c - "Most want PM elected direct," Dan Izenberg, p.2.

10/3/90 - "New private facility opens in Haifa," Judy Siegel-Itzkovitch, p.9.

10/17/90 - "IMA mum on how much doctors make," Judy Siegel, p.2.

C) *Ma'ariv:*

6/14/88 - "Worth, and Worth More," Shlomo Ness, pp.12–13.

2/9/90a - "The Second Channel. Who is it good for and for whom is it less good?" Esther Goldbarsht, p.1c.

2/9/90b - "Democracy Going to the Dogs," Yitzchak Ben-Khorin, pp.6–10 [Weekend Magazine].

D) *Yediot Akhronot:*

4/6/90 - "The Number of Hunger Strikers Has Reached 12; Thousands Have Turned to the President: Change the System," Zvi Singer & Gabi Baron, p.2.

E) *The New York Times:*

4/6/90 - "Political Deal-Making Angers Israelis," Joel Brinkley, p.A4.

4/11/90 - "Peres and Allies to Form Government," Joel Brinkley, p.A3.

F) *Business Week:*

6/5/89 - "The Paradox of *Perestroika*: A Raging Black Market," Peter Galuszka, p.66, 70.

Index

ment/organization/group, 13, 52, 127, 133, 134, 147, 148, 154; politician, 90; potential revolts, 139–50; pressure, 28, 29, 49, 51, 67, 111, 113, 129, 131, 133, 134; revolt, 1, 3, 4, 6, 7, 8, 9, 36, 39, 41, 45, 48, 49, 51, 53, 54, 55, 60, 62, 66, 67, 69, 70, 71, 72, 73, 75, 77, 78, 79, 80, 81, 82, 83, 85, 87, 89, 91, 93, 94, 99, 109, 111, 116, 117, 118, 119, 120, 121, 122, 123, 125, 126, 127, 128, 135, 136, 139, 145, 151, 152, 154, 156, 159, 162, 165, 169, 171, 172, 173, 174, 175; relationship, 130; self-help, 140, 141, 158; solutions, 113, 136; spirit, 90, 103, 169; voluntary committees, 157

Grupper, Pessah, 175
Guns, 149
Gurr, Ted, 161
Gush Dan, 146
Gush Emunim, 59, 60, 61, 62, 63, 64, 65, 145: Amanah, 145

Ha'aretz, 92, 93
Haifa, 101, 146, 148, 175
Halevy, Haim David, 118
Halper, Jeff, 106
Hanke, Steve, 18, 70, 71, 82, 83
Ha'shomer Ha'tzair, 15
Health, 97–104, 148, 159, 174: accreditation, 97; Black Medicine, 99, 101, 102, 103, 175; care, 54, 71, 99, 100, 101, 103; clinics, 97, 101, 103; doctors, 98, 99, 100, 101, 102, 103, 120; education, 120; emergency, 101; expenditure, 100; grey medicine, 99, 100; Hadassah Medical School, 100; Herzliyah Medical Center, 100, 102; hospitals, 50, 97, 98, 100, 101, 102, 103, 104, 120; infant mortality, 97; insurance, 101, 104; *Kupat Cholim Clalit* (KCC), 30, 78, 97, 98, 99, 100, 101, 102, 103, 104; Maccabi, 100; nurs-

es, 98; operation, 98, 99, 100, 101, 102; patients, 98, 99, 100, 101, 102, 103, 120; plans, 99, 104; private, 100, 101, 103, 120, 172; reform, 98, 103, 104; Sheba Hospital, 103; social welfare worker, 120; State Judicial Commission, 103; tax, 103; technology, 80. *See also* Histadrut

Health Ministry, 97, 98, 101, 102, 103, 104, 147: Comptroller's Report, 98
Hebrew, 127
Herut. *See* Likud
Herzl, Theodore, 13, 20: tomb of, 125
Hirschman, Albert, 82, 162, 163, 164, 166
Histadrut, 15, 16, 18, 19, 25, 26, 29, 30, 33, 37, 41, 46, 70, 80, 81, 94, 98, 101, 104, 156: elections, 47; health system, 97, 100; Labor establishment, 46; Koor, 46; Solel Boneh, 46; trade union, 97
Hitler, Adolf, 37
Holland, 80
Housing, 24, 51, 73: apartments, 88; mortgage, 149; old age, 81; prices, 149; rent strike, 149; shortage, 141; zoning, 141
Hungary, 174

Immigrants. *See* Aliyah
Individualism, 13
Interior Ministry, 23, 30, 118, 119, 157
International Monetary Fund (IMF), 69
Intifada, 66, 141–42, 143, 144, 145
Ireland, 69
Israel/Israeli, 28, 47, 50, 51, 54, 55, 60, 62, 64, 66, 67, 69, 72, 75, 76, 77, 79, 81, 82, 86, 87, 88, 93, 94, 98, 100, 101, 106, 110, 111, 114, 115, 116, 118, 119, 121, 122, 123, 124, 125, 126, 127, 129, 139, 142, 144, 145, 146, 147, 148, 149, 150, 151, 152, 153, 154, 155, 156, 157, 158,